# BRIGHT IDEAS

# Inspirations for CROSS-CURRICULAR THEMES

Published by Scholastic
Publications Ltd,
Villiers House,
Clarendon Avenue,
Leamington Spa,
Warwickshire CV32 5PR

© 1993 Scholastic Publications Ltd

Written by Alistair Ross
Edited by Felicity Kendall
Sub-edited by Magdalena Hernas
Designed by Keith Martin and
Micky Pledge
Series designed by Juanita
Puddifoot
Illustrated by Catherine Ward
Cover design by Micky Pledge
Cover artwork by Nick Ward


Designed using Aldus Pagemaker
Processed by Pages Bureau,
Leamington Spa
Artwork by David Harban Design,
Warwick


Printed in Great Britain by
Ebenezer Baylis & Son, Worcester

**British Library Cataloguing in
Publication Data**
A catalogue record for this book is
available from the British Library.

ISBN 0-590-53029-1

# CONTENTS

# INTRODUCTION

# Introduction

Cross-curricular teaching has played an exciting and invigorating part in the primary school tradition for many years. Integrated approaches to learning have taken the child's holistic view of the world seriously, as a way of synthesising knowledge and understanding about the world. This approach to teaching has also had its critics, who pointed out the problems of trying to integrate everything – the 'how-do-we-fit-some-music-and-RE-into-our-topic-on-colour' syndrome.

The idea of cross-curricularity has now developed beyond this, to the stage where we need to address 'the whole curriculum' for our children. This idea of the whole curriculum is much wider than the formal definitions of a National Curriculum and addresses areas that cover several of the component disciplines or subjects; indeed, it has been defined as everything that is taught and learned in school.

As teachers, we know that children learn much more in school than what is formally taught. For example, the way that some people use gender-specific language and have, unconsciously, different expectations for boys and girls, has been one of the factors contributing to children developing stereotypes of women's and men's roles. These sorts of unpredicted outcomes are sometimes described as 'the hidden curriculum'.

In England and Wales there is a formally defined National Curriculum, while in Scotland the Review and Development Group on Assessment and the Curriculum 5-14 has produced a broadly similar prescription. A number of subjects are directed for study, but the Education Reform Act of 1988 also requires schools to give children 'a broad and balanced curriculum', of which the National Curriculum is only a part. The National Curriculum Council strongly suggest that the use of particular cross-curricular themes is the most useful way to do this and recommend that all primary schools should address five particular themes:
• education for economic and industrial understanding;
• health education;
• careers education and guidance;
• environmental education;
• education for citizenship.

# BACKGROUND

The Education Reform Act of 1988 sought to offer all children 'an entitlement' to a 'broad and balanced' curriculum. Schools were expected to ensure that all children were taught both a wide range of curricular activities and a curriculum that did not emphasise some subjects at the expense of others. It was made very clear in the Act that the National Curriculum alone did not provide a broad and balanced curriculum. The legislation made a distinction between the 'whole curriculum' (broad and balanced, which all schools are obliged to provide) and the 'basic curriculum' (those parts that are described and defined in the Statutory Orders – the National Curriculum with Religious Education).

The best way to visualise these rather confusing requirements is as a set of subjects. Figure 1 shows the essential pattern. At the centre lies the set of core subjects – mathematics, English and science. These are, of course, also within the set of foundation subjects, which includes, for primary schools, technology, geography, history, art, music and PE. The core and other foundation subjects make up the National Curriculum. These subjects are defined in the Act and their content is described in the statutory instruments through programmes of study and attainment targets.

The basic curriculum also includes religious education, the provision of which is compulsory, but the content of which is fixed by the local Standing Advisory Committees on Religious Education. The Act goes on to say that the whole curriculum is greater than the basic curriculum, and that the National Curriculum Council should inform schools of the areas and issues that must be addressed in this 'gap' between the two.

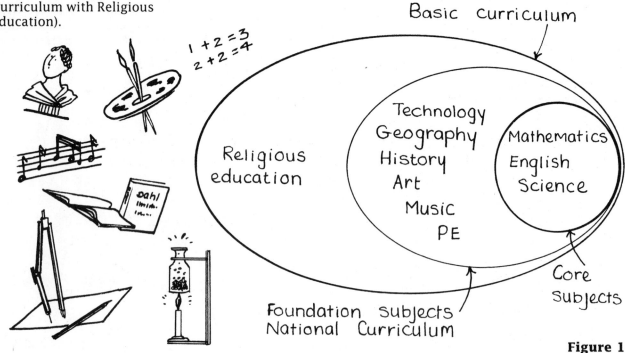

Figure 1

In Scotland, the Education Reform Act does not apply, so the terminology is rather different. Nevertheless, the same requirement for breadth and balance in the curriculum applies, and the 5-14 Review and Development Group on the Curriculum has worked in a broadly similar way to define the characteristics of the whole curriculum.

The National Curriculum Council produced a definition of the whole curriculum in their publication *Curriculum Guidance 3: The Whole Curriculum* (1990). This suggested that cross-curricular elements that were not specifically addressed in the basic curriculum should be included as ingredients in the whole curriculum. Figure 2 below shows this extended conception of the whole curriculum. Three elements are described, each of which is further subdivided into cross-curricular dimensions, cross-curricular skills and cross-curricular themes.

### Cross-curricular dimensions

These permeate and inform the delivery of all elements of the curriculum. These dimensions concern major social policies directed at ensuring equality of opportunity for all in our society:
• equal opportunities for males and females;
• equal recognition of cultural, linguistic and ethnic diversity;
• consideration of each individual's special needs.

### Cross-curricular skills

There are a number of high-level skills that can be developed and exercised across many areas of the curriculum:
• communication,
• numeracy,
• study skills,
• problem-solving skills,
• personal and social skills,
• information-technology handling skills.

These skills are not dependent on a particular subject-based content, but can and should be used by children in all of their work where relevant.

### Cross-curricular themes

These are areas of experience which link together several different subjects within the curriculum; they often include parts of other subjects that are not mentioned in the National Curriculum. The National Curriculum Council has identified five of these, all

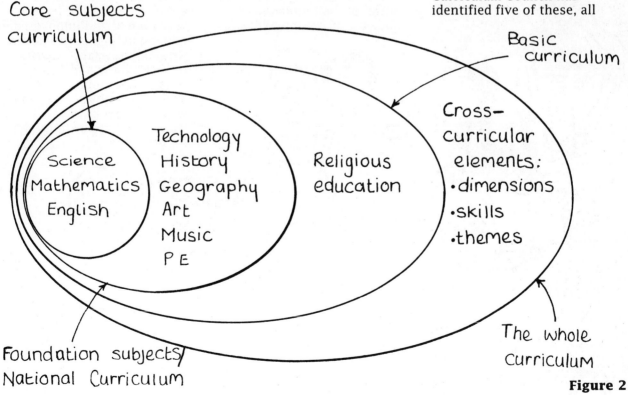

**Figure 2**

covering Key Stages 1 to 4, and published booklets on each of them in the Curriculum Guidance series:
• *Education for Economic and Industrial Understanding* (1990)
• *Health Education* (1990)
• *Careers Education and Guidance* (1990)
• *Environmental Education* (1990)
• *Education for Citizenship* (1990)

These are, of course, not the only possible cross-curricular themes, but together with the other elements of the whole curriculum, they provide opportunities for children to explore and understand a wide range of concepts, attitudes and knowledge that are commonly seen as important in understanding life today.

One cynical definition of the cross-curricular themes might be 'those bits of a possible curriculum that the Government forgot about when it was compiling the National Curriculum list of foundation subjects in June 1987!' However, there do seem to be a number of important aspects that they have in common:
• they link different forms of knowledge;
• they are of importance to human activity;
• they concern controversial issues, rather than those simply of fact.

## Linking areas of knowledge

Each cross-curricular theme uses some of the content, ways of working or concepts of several of the foundation subjects. For example, health education draws upon some of the content of the science curriculum, some of the process in physical education, and uses oral aspects of the English curriculum; it recognises the ways in which scientific knowledge can help us understand our health, but also shows some of the uses and limitations of science.

Cross-curricular themes do not necessarily cover all the foundation subjects, nor should they attempt to do so in an unnecessarily forced way. Cross-curricularity is concerned with recognising and enhancing existing and real links, not about manufacturing relationships simply for the sake of it.

Each cross-curricular theme offers important ways of perceiving how it is useful, and often essential, to examine problems and issues from a variety of perspectives. Without this cross-curricular approach we would have a very limited and impoverished understanding. In this context we gain important insights into the usefulness and nature of science, geography, history and the social sciences, which we would not have had without the opportunity that forged these links.

## Importance to human activity

There are five themes that predominate in the various British educational systems and these are of major significance in developing children's understanding of their world.

*Economic and industrial understanding* concerns issues of how we organise the exchange of goods and services, not simply market forces, but a complex interchange between producers, consumers and the public interest; how we decide to allocate our scarce resources; and how we organise our workplaces, and for whose benefit. These are important areas in which children need to develop a very real sense of critical understanding.

*Health education* is an area of major concern as we come to realise that preventive health care and a general awareness of health-related issues provide an essential complement to the treatment-led approach to health care that has dominated our thinking to date. Issues of diet, exercise, family and sexual relationships are fundamental to health, and have to be explored in terms of general education for all, rather than as specialist areas for those with particular interests in the health-related professions.

*Careers education and guidance* can be seen as perhaps the odd theme out in relation to primary children. Nevertheless, children in the primary years are already developing an important sense of self and self-esteem, and measuring these expectations against a variety of careers. Studies on the choices primary children seem to be making towards eventual career choice display frightening gender biases. Too many boys and girls are ruling themselves out of possible careers at too early an age.

*Environmental education* deals with vital issues of global concern which children (and adults) must understand if we want to plan for the future. The growing shortage of non-renewable resources, the destruction of species of plants and animals, rising levels of pollution, the depletion of the ozone layer and global warming could scarcely not be major issues of concern. Again, finding a response is not the responsibility of specialists, 'environmentalists' and scientists: they may help suggest courses of action and specific remedies, but much of the solution will depend on all of us making conscious efforts to change our everyday behaviour.

*Citizenship* is an issue that affects us all. Growing up in increasingly complex and interdependent societies, young people must learn to co-operate and negotiate in a peaceful manner. Despite the term 'citizenship' having overtones of charters and the like, this area is essentially one of learning how to behave politically – to achieve agreement on action despite differing needs and viewpoints. There is much research evidence to suggest

that the foundation of political understanding and of citizenship are laid down in the early years of schooling.

In many of these areas we may have experts with specialist knowledge and skills (economists, doctors, nurses, scientists, politicians) who can sometimes take a lead. But it is also essential that everyone else has a sound understanding and appreciation of the issues, and their impact on everyday lives.

## Controversial issues

The cross-curricular themes are generally not concerned with clear-cut matters of fact. In many of the issues involved there are substantial differences of opinion about

how the issue should be approached, the correct course of action and what the possible outcome might be. Most of these areas are surrounded by ongoing public debates. In identifying these themes, we are saying that children are entitled to have access to these debates. They ought to be allowed to see why people differ in their opinions, and to differentiate between opinion, self-interest and objective enquiry. Children ought to develop an attitude of critical enquiry: they should not accept without question the views and opinions of

others (particularly others with vested interests), but should be able to raise questions of bias and controversy.

This is a difficult area, perhaps particularly for the teachers of primary children, as we have developed a school culture that tends to avoid areas of controversy. Children tend to be cocooned from some of the 'difficult' areas of the real world, at least in our schools. Of course, if we think about the whole range of information sources available to children today (far wider than it was even a generation ago), we realise that children have access to and an understanding of a very wide range of social issues. Often that understanding is less than perfect. This is because information sources can be partial, incomplete and biased, often not designed to develop understanding in children; but also because these are areas that we may ignore or play down in our schools. We need to develop sensitive ways to explore issues of controversy in schools.

## Curriculum organisation

It is universally acknowledged that the primary school curriculum is overloaded. When the National Curriculum was first put together, it seems to have been intended for the secondary teachers, each of whom would receive the single neat folder relevant to their subject. Nobody thought of the poor primary teacher, who would end up with nine volumes on her desk.

To add cross-curricular themes to the notion of the 'whole curriculum' might therefore seem like madness, piling yet more on the already overburdened teachers. The National Curriculum Council imply that the cross-curricular themes are merely a different way of presenting what is already present in the foundation subjects. This, however, may be an oversimplification, because the cross-curricular themes do introduce much that is new, in terms of content and approach. However, it is possible to see the notion of cross-curricularity, and these themes in particular, as a way of simplifying the organisation of the delivery of the curriculum. The themes can allow a more structured approach to project planning, that encompasses both the best traditions of primary practice, and the major elements of the new foundation subjects and their programmes of study.

There are three different ways of approaching the cross-curricular themes in the primary school.
• If you are adopting a largely subject-based approach to planning, it is possible to identify elements of each cross-curricular theme in each subject, and to use these to enliven subject teaching.
• If you have chosen a project- or topic-based approach to planning, it is probably even easier to find a raft of elements of cross-curricular themes that can be used to illuminate each project or topic.
• Finally, it is possible to make a project or topic revolve around an exploration of a cross-curricular theme, and to approach programmes of

study and foundation subjects through that theme.
This book is designed to accommodate all three approaches to planning, allowing the teacher and the school to select the form that best suits their children's needs. My own preference is for a combination of the second and third approach, but I know many primary teachers who have successfully adopted the subject-based approach.
Adding cross-curricular themes to a subject calls for a little lateral thinking. While every foundation subject probably has some relationship with every cross-curricular theme, these relationships will not be present in every part of every programme of study. So when a particular topic is being

approached, consider how secure the links are with each cross-curricular theme. For example, in mathematics, introducing geometrical shapes to Year 2 children might offer very few links with any of the themes; but data-handling and presentation, on the other hand, cries out to use information about real issues (traffic levels and pollution in environmental education, food intakes and diet in health education, controlling the stock in a school shop in industrial and economic understanding). The problem here is to select one theme that will best illustrate the points of data-handling.
Adding cross-curricular themes to a topic or project may be easier: the problems may be of too many possibilities, rather than too few. It might be wise to limit oneself to using only one or perhaps two of the themes in any one project. This would allow sufficient emphasis and clarity about the theme itself to emerge. Many topics and projects seem to suggest automatically an associated

theme – for example, 'The seasons' link with 'The environment', 'People who help us' with 'Careers', 'Shops' with 'Economic and industrial understanding', and so on. Begin to plan the project in your usual way and then consider how a particular cross-curricular theme might be interwoven into this. The juxtaposition of project and theme will often illuminate the principal learning points in the topic. It will be relatively easy to make connections between the cross-curricular theme you have chosen and most of the elements of the foundation subject that you have incorporated into the topic.

Using the cross-curricular theme as a starting point for project or topic work is not as bold or innovative a move as it might at first seem. There are a number of familiar topics that have their origins in cross-curricular themes, often in a quite explicit way. For example, the 1970s health education project *All About Me* (Schools Council) is probably the ancestor of many classroom projects that focus on 'Me', 'My body' or 'Ourselves'.

### Active learning

There are a variety of modes of teaching and learning, and current evidence on classroom organisation suggests that the successful teacher is one who adopts all these approaches,

mixing and changing modes to suit particular children's current learning needs, and the particular needs of parts of the curriculum. So, a mixture of whole-class, individual and group activities may be used across the day, changing from activity to activity.

Cross-curricular themes also require this variety. But, as has been noted above, the themes often deal with issues located in the real world, that are contentious in some way. Because of this peculiar nature of the themes, there are certain ways of organising learning that might be better than others.

First, much of the learning will be achieved through social interaction. This means encouraging children to share ideas and experiences through talk and discussion. The children will need to find out what their peers have experienced, what they think and why, and the best way to

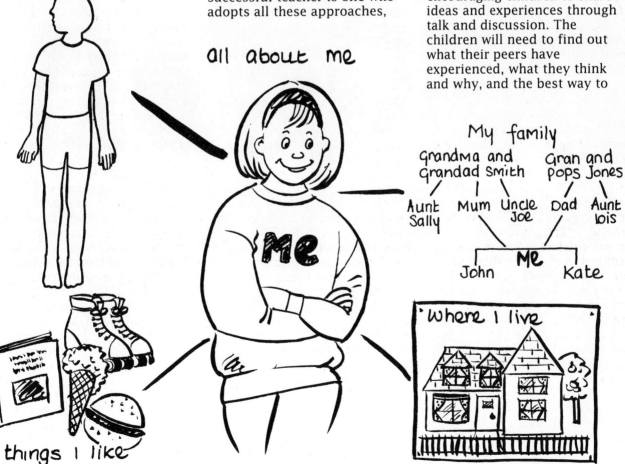

do this is to talk to them, in small or large groups. There is detailed guidance on the organisation of talk and discussion elsewhere in *Inspirations for Speaking and Listening* by Alistair Ross (1992) Scholastic.

Second, much will be learned through active investigation. Making enquiries, devising experiments, using senses of touch, taste, smell, sight and hearing will make learning more real and more permanent.

Third, because the issues are real and 'out there', a lot of learning will involve visiting. This need not mean major excursions – short visits in the locality will be sufficient to let the children gather observations about what people are doing and what is happening, capture it in some way (with a tape-recorder, a painting, a photograph or a piece of writing), and bring it back to the classroom to analyse, interpret and work on.

Finally, because many of the themes have an essential social content, good learning in the area of the cross-curricular themes will involve working with adults other than teachers. This does not mean that other adults substitute for the teacher, but that they are used as a resource for the children. Other adults can share experiences and views, express opinions, give life histories, demonstrate skills and pass on knowledge. The teacher could become an intermediary, collecting all this information for the children, filtering and classifying it before it is passed on; but it is much more effective for children to have direct contact with other adults, so that they learn skills of interacting with other people, learn how to ask questions, how to sift, sort and classify all the raw data. Children may learn more from seeing you as a learner (modelling themselves on how you join with them asking questions and how you find out with them) than if you pre-select all the facts that they receive.

## Planning and progression

It is difficult enough in schools today to plan across the

classes a coherent curriculum approach that ensures adequate coverage, continuity and progression. Adding cross-curricular themes may seem like adding to the potential for confusion.

One very useful starting point for schools may be to conduct an audit of the cross-curricular themes. This would mean looking back at the curriculum as it exists to identify where the themes are already touched upon. Many elements of the themes may be quite adequately dealt with in what is already planned or ongoing, but an audit will identify areas of need. An audit should also cover the resources that are available to support cross-curricular theme teaching. Some of these resources will be the straightforward human and physical resources of the school, for example, books and packs of materials, teachers and other adults with particular experiences. Other resources may be support bodies and networks. The local education authority may be a useful starting point, but there are other local and national environmental groups, education–business partnerships and so on, all of which can become resources in terms of ideas, materials and contacts. Not least, there are the resources of the local community, for example, shops, offices, businesses, local councils, newspapers, community and pressure groups and old people's homes.

Having conducted the audit, consider what the aims of the school should be in terms of the themes. What sort of balance and breadth are you hoping to achieve? What sort of contacts with the local community should the children have had by the time they are seven and by the time they are eleven?

From the audit and the aims, look next at the tactical steps necessary to achieve the aims. Are there particular themes or items on which you need to focus? At what point in the child's career through the school would they best be located? How does this relate to the existing curriculum plans?

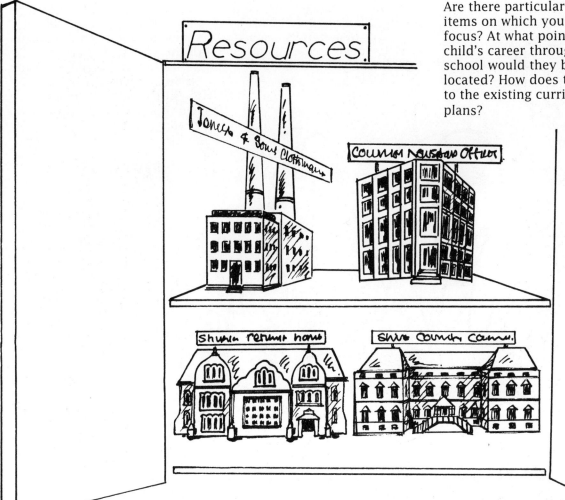

It is important that individual teachers know what the cross-curricular themes are first, and how they can be approached in the primary school, before the staff take on planning a whole-school approach. What ideas work best? Why?

## How to use this book

This book is organised around the five curriculum themes suggested by the National Curriculum Council. Each theme is treated in a separate chapter but this is not to suggest that the themes cannot be successfully integrated and combined. Not all themes are given equal attention: more space has been allocated to those that are both popular and most relevant to primary children's needs.

The introductory background section for each chapter outlines what the theme is about: the major ideas it explores, the areas of experience and knowledge that it encompasses and the suggestions that have been made of what learning is appropriate for different-aged children within the primary school. These introductions offer important frameworks for each of the themes: they will make clear what is only implicit in the activities that follow.

In each of the five chapters, the introduction is followed by a number of activities. Each activity suggests the age range for which it is best suited.

However, this is only an indication as it is generally possible to modify most activities to fit any age across the primary school. There is also a suggestion for how the activity might be linked to aspects of foundation subjects: this will make it easy to use for those teachers who have adopted a subject-based approach. Activities are also supported by indications of the materials needed and by possible extension or development activities.

The last chapter outlines a range of project-based approaches to the various cross-curricular themes. These charts indicate how aspects of each theme might be developed as a project or topic in its own right. There is not space to include all the details of the project, but broad indications are given of what might be included and how it might develop. In most cases, two topics are developed, for younger and for older children.

# CHAPTER 1

# Economic and industrial awareness

At first sight, industry and the economy might seem far removed from the world of the primary school. But children are aware of many of the economic aspects of what is going on around them. They are consumers in their own right, increasingly having the opportunity to make decisions about spending and responding to advertising directed at them. They see people buying and selling in the shops; money being passed across the counter, out of cash dispensers, from post offices. They also see and hear about important financial events on television, some of which may affect their families.

More families still are affected by work, or the lack of it. From a very early age children are aware of adults in their family either at work, or aspiring to be at work. They see people working on the street, in shops, at surgeries and schools. Industry is not solely concerned with manufacturing: the term also includes services, retailing, distribution, local government, farming and food processing.

Young children are no novices in economic and industrial understanding, but on many occasions they are left to make sense of these experiences on their own. While this is valuable in itself, children need help to interpret the economic aspects of the world about them. This is what the theme 'economic and industrial awareness' aims to do.

# BACKGROUND

Economic and industrial understanding combines two elements:
• the traditional academic discipline of economics;
• the industrial location for particular types of economic, social, managerial and other activities.

This dual approach reflects the origins of the theme: it springs from the work with primary schools in the schools-industry area in the 1980s, and from the 'Economic awareness' curriculum development project of the late 1980s. Both sets of activities showed quite convincingly that not only can primary children learn successfully about these areas, but that, because of the frequent misconceptions and because of the significance of the subject matter, these themes needed to cover both primary and secondary education.

## The child's viewpoint

We know quite a bit about children's ideas about money and work. Often children's explanations are seen as comic misunderstandings and are used to demonstrate their inability to cope with seemingly too sophisticated notions. But when one examines them in more detail, it can often be seen that they are attempts to offer sensible explanations based on partial observations, or generalisations based on particular incidents.

For example, if young children are asked whether a greengrocer will sell oranges for more, less or the same price as he bought them wholesale, a substantial number of five-year-olds suggest that he will sell them for less than the price for which he bought them. This is sometimes used as evidence that children of this age can have no understanding of the idea of buying and selling. But if these children are asked why this is so, they often explain their answer by pointing out that the oranges will be second-hand. Second-hand goods are cheaper – this is often part of a child's real experience. Few children will have had any experience of buying and selling goods in a greengrocer's shop, and so what most children seem to do is to transfer the experience that they are familiar with (second-hand buying and selling) to the unfamiliar context of the oranges.

Similarly, when asked where money comes from, young children suggest that it is given to people in shops – the shopper gives a little to the shopkeeper, but the

shopkeeper gives more back to the shopper. This has been used by some researchers to suggest that such children are at a pre-concrete stage in which they have no concept of the nature or function of money, and see shopping as a 'ritual exchange' of money. The explanation may, however, be simpler. These children are probably using the term 'money' in a very straightforward manner, to mean coins. In shops, customers tend to give notes or a few high-value coins, and receive as change a greater number of low-value coins. If we define money as coins, then the children are quite correct – nearly all the coins we have in our purses and pockets have been 'given' to us in shops. (Banknotes, of course, come from holes in the wall!)

## Economic understanding

Economics is about how decisions to allocate scarce resources are made. We all make decisions about how we use time, money and space, so we all behave economically, trying to get the best value from our decisions. What we mean by the term 'value' may vary: it is not always about maximising our personal wealth. Frequently people make decisions that give them less wealth but more of something else that they value more highly, or make decisions that they feel benefit

someone other than themselves.

Economics has had rather a bad press in recent years – many people see it as being solely concerned with the use of free markets to arrive at 'true' values or prices. Some economic thinkers stress monetarist values and some assume that everyone acts (or should act) in a wholly rational way. But economics is wider than this: many decisions we make that are not simply market-led have a strong economic element.

The following example will help illustrate this. A young teacher has a choice of how to spend her summer holiday: she can either take a four-week package holiday in the Mediterranean or spend the time redecorating her flat. This is a choice largely concerning the scarce resource of time: she cannot do both activities, because school starts again in September. The 'cost' of the holiday is having to continue to live in a poorly-decorated flat for at least a few more months, because it is the chance to change this that is

forgone by going to Spain. This is known as the 'opportunity cost': the equivalent opportunity cost of redecorating is not having four weeks of sun and Mediterranean food.

There are, of course, some other costs that can also be considered: the cost of decorating materials, the cost of the holiday, the comparative living expenses at home and abroad. But ultimately, it depends on the subjective value the teacher places on each of the alternatives.

We are all making decisions of an economic nature all the time and most adults have considerable everyday experiences of how the economy works. For example, taking out a loan or a mortgage, arranging insurance, following currency fluctuations when abroad, deciding what type of building society account to open and managing a household budget, all require an understanding of the complexities of money and finance, and most of us manage these tolerably well. While these are adult skills, their origins can begin to develop in the primary school. They are everyday survival skills that children will need in order to survive in contemporary society.

## The range of industry

Industry is a wide-ranging concept. Ask a group of adults or children to draw a picture to represent industry and at least some of them will depict tall smoking chimneys and rows of sloping factory roofs. This stereotype extends to representations of managers (invariably male, middle-aged and white, pinstripe suit, briefcase, bowler). One group of children who had worked over a period of weeks with a young woman manager, and who had never met any other manager, still drew men in suits when asked this question! Stereotypical images, however, are sometimes drawn because it is an easy way to quickly make a point: they do not necessarily reflect the views of the person expressing them.

We use the word 'industry' in a whole variety of different contexts, and simply looking at the range of these industrial settings demonstrates the enormous breadth of industry in our lives:
• primary industry includes all forms of mining and quarrying, and farming;
• secondary or manufacturing industry includes a wide range of activities which involve making things;
• tertiary industry includes both freight and passenger traffic, building houses and roads, domestic housework, banking and accountancy, tourism, catering, garages, window-cleaning, local government, hospitals and schools, shops and supermarkets.

## Economic behaviour

We all have experiences of the economy in our everyday lives. But we can also each have several different

economic roles as the consumer, producer and economic regulator. This can be a useful way of thinking about the sorts of economic experiences children should be encountering.

### Consumer
The most common economic role that children have experienced is that of the *consumer*. It is during the primary years that they move from simply expressing wants and desires to making decisions about purchases, and responding to advertisements. They may not be spending large amounts, but most eleven-year-olds are in charge of spending about

two pounds a week. The attitudes and strategies they develop during this period will underpin much of their future learning as consumers. As well as making their own buying decisions, they also play an important part in influencing the decisions of their parents and guardians. Much advertising for clothes and footwear, for example, is directed at young children – not because the children themselves will necessarily make the purchase, but because they will exert pressure on their parents. Some of this advertising plays upon young people's desire to conform to peer groups, so that, for example, only the 'correct' designer labels for footwear are acceptable. Children also influence parents' supermarket buying,

and there are a variety of point-of-sale techniques designed to maximise the pressure children put on the adult customer.

What are the implications of this for the primary school teacher? Much can be done to increase children's awareness of how producers and advertisers are trying to manipulate them. One of the most important lessons for children is to learn to differentiate between needs and wants: to learn how to prioritise their possible purchases. Much, too, can be done to increase their critical awareness of advertisers. It seems that younger infant children see television advertising largely as moving wallpaper, something that interrupts the show, or indeed is part of it. But in the primary years that follow, they become first subject to the advertisers' charms, and then begin to develop critical strategies to deal with them. It can be

helpful to foster such strategies. Look carefully with them at a video recording of the Saturday morning television advertisements. Can they spot the hand holding the toy that appears to fly by itself and see the deceptive ways in which prices are shown on the screen? Advertisers are allowed to show several related products with, for example, the information that 'Prices range from £1.50 to £49.50'; so as long as one of the products shown is the cheapest item, most of the advertisement can concentrate on the more expensive one.

Another area in which to develop critical consumer awareness are supermarket layouts. Why are goods positioned where they are? At what height and for whom? Where will children be waiting in queues and getting bored?

Science and technology can be used in comparing different products to determine value for money and best buys. Can children taste the difference in blind tests? Does one washing-up liquid behave significantly better than another? What do the labels tell the consumer and why?

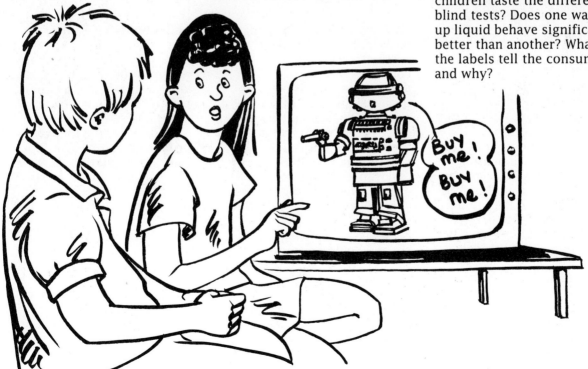

### Producer

A second major economic role, and one that children are, necessarily, less aware of, is that of the *producer*. Children in our society tend not to be producers and much of what adult producers do is usually hidden from children's eyes. Investigating how things are produced and how services are provided generally involves looking at particular workplaces and particular products. Starting points can be parents' workplaces, other

local workplaces or tracing back to its origins one of the products that children consume.

It can be surprising to discover just how little children know about where things come from and how they are produced. For example, in one study, several children independently explained that oranges were constructed in factories: the skins were made by condensing orange juice till it set and could be formed into casings, whereupon they were filled up with juice and despatched to the supermarket. It was a child of Spanish origin who had seen them growing on trees that put them right. This may sound

quaint, but millions of adults were taken in by an item on the TV programme *Tonight* in the late 1950s, which showed agricultural workers in Italy harvesting the spaghetti crop from trees (broadcast on April 1). Without experiences, discussion and investigation, it is easy to assume that many natural products are processed and vice versa (for example, plastic is extracted from mines).

Understanding the role of producers can be developed through simulation and role-playing, and several ideas later in this chapter explore techniques for this.

### Economic regulator

The two economic roles of consumers and producers are not enough. Left to themselves, the two groups will create a market (sometimes free, sometimes monopolistic) that may satisfy in various ways the needs of

both. Free-market economics often assumes that such 'perfect competition' will meet all needs and be a sufficient and indeed necessary regulator, allowing supplies to match demand. However, not everyone is party to every transaction and the community as a whole may need at times to intervene in the market, regulating freedom to trade in the wider interests of the community. So a third role, that of the citizen as an *economic regulator*, is also important.

The following example will illustrate this. A totally free market would allow any cigarette producer or retailer to trade with anyone to buy cigarettes. The price would be fixed by the market and cigarettes would bear no more sales tax than any other product. But society does not allow this to happen: the government intervenes, not allowing children to buy cigarettes because society feels that they have not the knowledge to start an addiction that will damage their health. The government imposes additional duties on tobacco to discourage purchasers, and restricts the

ways and places in which cigarettes are advertised. Society as a whole cannot afford to allow the market alone to control this trade. Another example might be in the trading between power suppliers and consumers: it is certainly cheaper to use power sources that cause atmospheric pollution. Society however, through governmental taxation and regulatory policies, tries to stop this happening, by for example, insisting that emissions are kept low and by imposing environmental taxes that 'make the polluter pay'.

## Skills and attitudes

The National Curriculum Council document *Curriculum Guidance 4: Education for Economic and Industrial Understanding* (1990), HMSO provides a series of useful starting points by listing some of the skills and attitudes that can be developed over the

years of compulsory schooling.

By the age of 16, it suggests, children will have the skills to be able to:
• collect, analyse and interpret economic and industrial data;
• think carefully about different ways of solving economic problems and making economic decisions;
• distinguish statements of fact and value in economic situations;
• communicate economic ideas accurately and clearly;
• establish working relationships with adults outside school;
• co-operate as part of a team in enterprise activities;
• lead and take the initiative;
• handle differences of

economic interest and opinion in a group;
• communicate effectively and listen to the views of others on economic and industrial issues.

Many, if not all, of these will be begun within the years of primary education.

The attitudes that the document suggests children need to develop are all firmly rooted in the primary years:
• an interest in economic and industrial affairs;
• respect for evidence and rational argument in economic contexts;
• concern for the use of scarce resources;
• a sense of responsibility for the consequences of their own economic actions, as individuals and members of groups;
• respect for alternative economic viewpoints and a willingness to reflect critically on their own economic views and values;
• sensitivity to the effects of economic choices on the environment;
• concern for human rights, as these are affected by economic decisions.

## Knowledge and understanding

The National Curriculum Council document makes a number of very specific suggestions for what children in both the infant and the junior years need to consider. While there has been some criticism and misinterpretation of these statements, the following summary and reformulation of the proposals may be a useful starting point for teachers and schools to consider the range of activities that are already provided, and whether these need supplementing in the future.

There are four broad areas that are covered:
• economic concepts (the basic ideas of scarcity, choice, values and decisions);
• business, industry and the world of work (examining the role of producers);
• consumers (examining the role of consumers);
• government, economy and society (the role of the citizen in regulating economic activity).

For each of these, several areas of investigation are suggested for each stage of primary education.

## Economic concepts

### Limited resources and opportunity cost
At the infant level, children could:
• identify and make decisions about resources (what resources are needed for an activity, which are best, what we mean by best).

**Menu**
baked potatoe
with cheese
—
hamburger
with chips
—
Jelly
or
apple

At the junior level, children could:
• understand some of the implications of limited resources (know that decisions have to be made, that this will have consequences for other people now and in the future);
• know that all decisions involve opportunity cost (understand that when one course of action is decided upon, the cost is what cannot now be done instead).

### Costs and benefits
At the infant level, children could:
• understand some of the costs and benefits in situations they are concerned with

(discuss making decisions, including what they will gain and lose in taking alternative courses of action).
    At the junior level, children could:
• understand costs and benefits in everyday economic choices, recognising that people can have different and conflicting interests.

### Needs and wants
At the infant level, children could:
• understand that people have needs (realise the basic necessities for life – food, warmth, shelter, security).
    At the junior level, children could:
• appreciate that human needs, unlike wants, are universal, and that for many people their needs are not met (distinguish between goods and services that may be desirable but not essential, and genuine necessities; and be aware of global inequalities in the distribution of necessities).

## Business, industry and the world of work

### Exchange
At the infant level, children could:
• know that buying, selling and giving are ways of exchanging goods and services (not all transactions are governed by price).
    At the junior level, children could:
• understand how money is used in some exchanges of goods and services, and know some of the factors that affect prices.

### Work and jobs
At the infant level, children could:
• know that there are different kinds of work and that these involve different skills (look at the jobs around them, the people who do them, and some of the skills and complexities of the tasks involved);
• know that people work in different kinds of workplaces and do different jobs (visit some local workplaces such as shops and the school kitchen, and discuss the differences among themselves and with the workers).

At the junior level, children could:
• understand that workplaces are organised in different ways (begin to look at differing roles of managers, supervisors and workers, look at forms of ownership and control);
• develop their understanding of the nature of work and of its place in people's lives (talk about why people work and the forms of satisfaction and dissatisfaction that it brings).

### Production, distribution and sale

At the infant level, children could:
• understand how some things are produced, using different resources.

At the junior level, children could:
• have some understanding of how goods are produced, distributed and sold (follow through goods from their origin to point of sale).

### Local workplaces

At the junior level, children could:
• know about public services, shops, offices and industries in their local community, and understand the importance of these to local people.

## Consumers

### Consumers and producers

At the infant level, children could:
• be aware that they are consumers, which links them to people who produce goods and provide services.

At the junior level, children could:
• understand what it means to be a consumer and how consumers and producers relate to each other.

## Government, economy and society

### Technological change

At the infant level, children could:
• understand how tools and technology contribute to their lives at home and at school.

At the junior level, children could:
• develop an awareness of the part played by design and technology in industrial production;
• be aware of some of the effects of the new technologies and their implications for people and places.

### Environmental issues

At the junior level, children could:
• appreciate some of the environmental and social issues associated with economic and industrial activity.

### Global issues

At the junior level, children could:
• recognise similarities and differences between economic and industrial activities in different parts of the world.

# ACTIVITIES

## 1. Needs and wants

### Foundation subject links
English, mathematics.

### Age range
Five to eleven.

### Group size
Groups of about six; some whole-class discussion.

### What you need
Newspapers and magazines with lots of advertisements for foodstuffs, household goods, furniture, cars, holidays and so on; four sheets of paper per group, glue, scissors, pencils.

### What to do
Ask the groups to look at each of the photographs in the advertisements in turn. For each item, they have to decide if it is something they absolutely must have in order to live, or if it is pretty useful, but not vital; or if they would like to have it but it is not really necessary; or if they simply are not interested.

As the children classify the items, they should list them on the sheets of paper or cut out the pictures and stick them on. The sheets could then be headed as follows:
• Things we have to have;
• Things we would find useful;
• Things we would like;
• Things we don't want.

You will need to explain that the categories should be looked at in order: if it is something they would like, as well as find essential, it goes in the 'Things we have to have' pile. If the children are not used to small-group negotiation, it might be easier to ask them to work in pairs. However, this is not an individual activity – children are supposed to argue about classifications and come to an agreement.

When several items have been grouped, bring the class together to discuss the findings so far, to see if there are any differences. Discuss what needs and wants are, and the differences between them.

### Further activity
Ask the groups or the whole class to discuss what the advertisers are trying to do. How do they present their products? (One of the advertisers' ploys is to try to make wants appear as needs.)

## 2. In scarce supply

### Foundation subject links
English, geography.

### Age range
Seven to eleven.

### Group size
Three to four; some whole-class discussion.

### What you need
Small pieces of card and felt-tipped pens (optional).

### What to do
Economists say that everything is scarce. By this they mean that quantities are limited and no one can have as much as they want. This is even true of commodities such as clean air and pure water. You may want to begin this activity with a short class discussion on the meaning of scarcity.

Ask each group to think about how scarce some of the following items are and how people get some of them:
• paper,
• burgers,
• money,
• pure water,
• television sets,
• television programmes,
• teachers,
• speciality dolls (for example, Barbie or Action Man type),
• packets of stickers (as bought in sweet shops).

Ask the children to consider the following questions:

• How is this item divided up?
• Is it difficult to get?
• Are there lots in the world?
• Are there lots around here?

You may want to write the name of each item on a small card, and to give one card at a time to each group. Try to ensure that several groups discuss the same item.

When each group has discussed a few items, bring them together to exchange their ideas. What is 'scarce' locally? What is abundant? How does this compare with other places in the world? How do people get hold of things that are scarce?

### Further activity
Add more items to the list, perhaps things that are currently popular with the children. Discuss if price and value are connected with scarcity or with each other.

# 3. Who gets what

### Foundation subject links
Mathematics, art.

### Age range
Seven to eleven.

### Group size
Individuals and small groups; some whole-class discussion.

### What you need
Modelling clay, card, scissors, glue, photocopiable page 167.

### What to do
Visit a local workplace, for example a hospital, a department store or a library with the class or a group. Encourage the children to ask the employees if they think they are fairly paid for what they do. Ask the personnel office for a list of pay scales for different categories of workers.

In class, ask children to make models of some of the people they have talked with. Ask each child (or each small group) to make a cardboard base for their model, with the height representing the average wage of a person of that grade (use a scale like 1cm=£1,000 a year, or 2cm=£25 a week). When they have finished, they should put each model on its plinth.

Discuss the results. Is is fair that some people get paid so much more than others? Why are they paid different amounts?

### Further activity
Ask the children to rank different workers according to what they think the workers ought to be paid. They could draw pictures of each worker on the steps on photocopiable page 167, and compare and discuss in groups the different results.

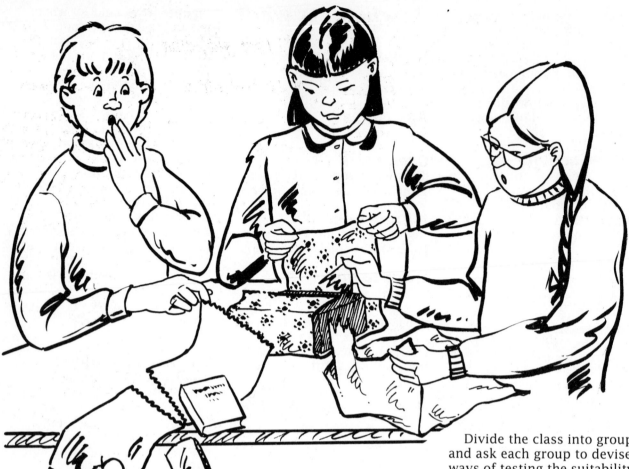

# 4. Best quality paper

### Foundation subject links
Technology, English.

### Age range
Five to eleven.

### Group size
Groups of up to six.

### What you need
A range of different types of paper, for example, drawing paper, wrapping paper, kitchen-roll and thin card; various materials normally used with each type of paper, for example, a variety of pencils, pens and paints; string, tape and a small box to wrap; containers for measuring out liquid to mop up; back issues of *Which?* magazine.

### What to do
Ask the class which is the best quality paper. When they have made a few suggestions, ask what will happen if they use these for inappropriate activities, for example, mopping up spilled liquids with drawing paper. Discuss with the children the range of uses paper has.

Divide the class into groups and ask each group to devise ways of testing the suitability of various kinds of paper for a particular task such as wrapping parcels. Ask the groups to test several types of paper (they need not all do this at the same time). How do they ensure that their tests are fair?

Ask the groups to prepare a short report or a demonstration of their findings. Which is the best paper for the job? What does it cost? Is it relatively cheap? If it is more expensive, is it worth the extra money?

### Further activity
Show the children old copies of *Which?* magazine. Can they make up a similar report? Could they come up with other 'best buys' for classroom materials?

# 5. In the card factory

## Foundation subject links
Technology, English.

## Age range
Nine to eleven.

## Group size
The whole class, divided into two groups.

## What you need
Paper, felt-tipped pens, photocopiable page 168.

## What to do
This activity compares a simulated production line with people working individually.

Explain how the 'Get well soon' card on photocopiable page 168 is made. There are several stages:
• folding the paper (A4 size folded twice to A6);
• drawing the design;
• colouring the design using felt-tipped pens in three different colours;
• writing the message on the front;
• writing the message inside.

Divide the class into two. One half, who will be working as a group, will need to arrange their tables in a long line. Ask them to sit in a production line and allocate the tasks, for example, one child folding; three children drawing (stage 1); three children drawing (stage 2); two children adding the first colour; two children adding the second colour; two children adding the third colour; one child writing the front messages; and one child writing the inside messages. Children in the second group will be making similar cards, but will work on their own.

Allow both groups to work for the same length of time. Then stop and discuss the results with the whole class. Which group has made the largest number of cards? Which group's cards look the most uniform? Which look the most individualistic or the most interesting? Who was able to talk with their friends as they worked? Who wants to take a card home? If they had to pay themselves a wage, and it was the same wage for everyone, what would each group/individual have to charge for each card? Is the difference in price between the individually made cards and the production-line cards worth it?

## Further activity
This activity can be adapted to make different cards at different seasons as appropriate, as well as Christmas or other seasonal decorations.

# 6. Cake bakers

### Foundation subject links
Technology (food), mathematics, English.

### Age range
Five to eleven.

### Group size
Six to ten, although it can be done by the whole class.

### What you need
Ingredients and utensils for baking cakes and an oven; materials for making advertisements (paper, paint, paintbrushes, crayons, felt-tipped pens).

### What to do
A group of children (perhaps the whole class) should form a mini-enterprise, making cakes for sale to the rest of the school and to parents or for a school fair. The emphasis is on the children taking the initiative and making their own decisions as much as possible. These are some of the questions that will arise at different points during this activity.
• Will the group of children have a name? What will it be?
• What do they need? (Recipes, ingredients)
• How will they get them? (Buy, borrow, ask for gifts)
• How much money do they need? How will they get it? (Loan, gift, pocket money)
• Who are they selling to? What do they want? (Market research)
• How will the cakes be sold? At what price? How will the customers know?

• Who will do what?
• What sort of records do they need to keep?
   Try to make the activity as realistic as possible: raise questions, rather than supply answers. The activity may spread over several days.

# 7. Who's in charge?

### Foundation subject links
English, geography (human).

### Age range
Seven to eleven.

### Group size
Individuals or the whole class.

### What you need
Card, coloured felt-tipped pens, scissors, thread, small garden canes (optional), adhesive, a large sheet of paper (optional).

### What to do
Take the class to visit a local workplace, for example, a supermarket or a hospital. Ask the children to talk with as

many different workers as possible (from a range of departments and including people at different managerial, supervisory and 'shop-floor' positions). The children could be encouraged to ask questions such as 'Who tells you what to do?' and 'Do you tell anyone else what to do?'.

Back in class, tell the children to list all the people that they spoke with and their respective jobs. Ask each child to draw a small picture of one of the workers on card, colour it and write the person's name at the bottom of the picture. (It may help to ask the children to make all the drawings approximately the same height.) The children should then cut out the figures.

Ask the whole class to discuss how they could arrange the figures to show who is in charge. The children should use the information they have collected to create a hierarchy of the workplace, showing the lines of management and the different departments. Discuss how systems like this work.

Then, either ask the children to stick the figures in place on a large sheet of paper, drawing in connecting lines; or use the figures to create a hanging mobile, using garden cane for the horizontal lines and thread for the vertical lines. (Making a mobile calls for some time and patience. Get the balance by working upwards, rather than down from the top!)

### Further activity
Discuss hierarchies in other workplace, such as the school.

# 8. Setting up home

### Foundation subject links
Mathematics, English.

### Age range
Seven to eleven, but could be adapted for younger children.

### Group size
Four to six.

### What you need
Mail order catalogues, a local newspaper with small ads for second-hand household goods, paper and pencils.

### What to do
Tell each group that they are to set up their own home. They already have the building, which they now have to furnish for themselves. They have no more than £1,000 to spend. What do they need, what does it cost and where will they get it from?

Give the children some time to work out what they think they need and to find it in the catalogues and small ads. They will need to discuss their needs and wants, and to look for the cheapest possible alternatives. You could point out, if asked, that £1,000 is for furnishing the house – the children should assume that money to buy food and other basic requirements is also available. Prompt them if necessary – sheets, light bulbs, cooking utensils....

Different groups could eventually compare their lists and priorities.

### Further activity
Discuss needs, wants and priorities with the class.

# 9. Out of stock

### Foundation subject links
Mathematics, English, technology, geography.

### Age range
Five to eleven.

### Group size
Two to three and the whole class.

### What you need
Materials for a class shop – try to concentrate on lots of packages for a small range of products; a till, toy money, shopping baskets, a telephone, paper, pencils.

### What to do
Set up a class shop. Some children will work in the shop, others will be customers. Roles will need to alternate over time. This class shop is different from others in that it is rather more realistic.

Encourage the shoppers to go in with particular goods in mind. If they are not in stock, they could complain to the manager. If goods run out, tell the manager she or he must order some more, rather than simply empty the shoppers' baskets to restock the shelves – that would not go down too well in their local supermarket!

The manager might use the phone to ring the warehouse (or a customer might suggest this). You could act in role as the warehouse supervisor, or deliver the goods and insist that you are paid for them, there and then.

Call round for the rent or send the shop an electricity bill. Try to build up the ideas that shops need to plan what they buy and to set money aside to meet the costs of their materials and overheads. Can the children find some way to keep track of what stock they have left? Can they afford to order much more stock that they will sell quickly? (You could turn into the Environmental Health Officer and check the use-by dates!)

### Further activity
Visit a real supermarket with the class or invite the local supermarket manager to school. Ask the children to discuss the problems they have had in running their shop. Do real-life managers have the same problems? What solutions do they have?

# 10. Supermarket plan

### Foundation subject links
Technology, English.

### Age range
Seven to eleven.

### Group size
Groups of four.

### What you need
Squared paper, felt-tipped pens in different colours, rulers, coloured paper, scissors.

### What to do
Draw a large rectangle on the squared paper to represent the ground plan of a supermarket. Tell the children what scale it is.

Ask them to plan the interior to sell as many goods as possible. They can use the coloured paper to cut out shapes representing shelves, frozen food cabinets, trolley parks, tills and so on, and move these around to find the best arrangement. Remind them to allow room for the shoppers to move about.

When they have planned the layout, ask them to decide where to put the different products. How do supermarkets make such decisions?

Ask different groups to compare their results. What was similar in their designs? What was different? Why were particular goods displayed as they are?

### Further activity

Invite the local supermarket manager to school to examine the plans and to offer comments. Encourage the children to ask how supermarket managers decide where to put different items. Send the plans to the supermarket chain's design department and invite them to comment (or even to visit the school); or offer to display the plans in the local supermarket.

# 11. Pot-a-plant

### Foundation subject links

Science, mathematics, English.

### Age range

Seven to eleven (in a modified form with older infants).

### Group size

Six to ten, or the whole class.

### What you need

Flowerpots, potting soil, seeds and cuttings.

### What to do

A group of children (perhaps the whole class) should form a mini-enterprise growing pot plants for sale. These could be sold at a school fair to parents and visitors. The emphasis is on the children taking the initiative and making their own decisions as much as possible.

Growing plants takes some time: it will be necessary to plan carefully in advance to make sure that the plants are properly grown (and not overgrown) by the time of the sale. Or, if the children decide to sell the plants over a period of time, planting should be staggered to get a spread of plants ready at different times.

The children will need to make a variety of decisions. These are some of the questions that will arise at different points in the course of this activity.

• Will the group have a name? What will it be?
• Who will do what?
• What do they need? (Pots, soil, cuttings and seeds)
• How will they get these? (Buy or borrow)
• How much money do they need? How will they get it? (It is possible to get small loans from the local bank for such mini-enterprise projects.)
• Who will buy the plants? What sort of plants do they want? How much are they prepared to pay? (Market research)

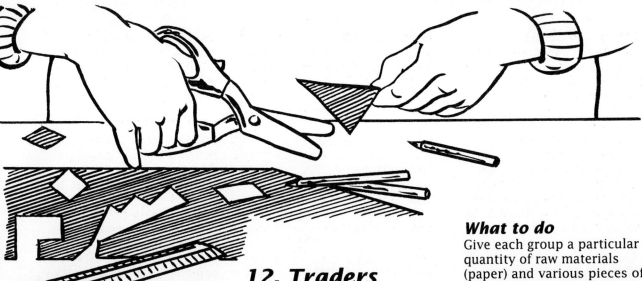

# 12. Traders

### Foundation subject links
Mathematics, English, geography.

### Age range
Seven to eleven.

### Group size
The whole class, divided into five or six groups.

### What you need
Scrap paper (plain on one side), pencils, rulers, scissors, money tokens, photocopiable page 169.

• How will the plants be sold? How will they be advertised? How will the customers know?
• What sort of records do they need to keep?

Try to make the activity as realistic as possible: raise questions, rather than supply answers. The activity will need to be spread over several weeks.

### What to do
Give each group a particular quantity of raw materials (paper) and various pieces of machinery (scissors, rulers and pencils). Each group represents a country with different quantities of these, and they all have to try to produce useful goods, by making as many of the shapes on photocopiable page 169 as they can. Finished goods (which must be accurately made) can be cashed at the bank. The teacher acts as the bank. The bank might also sell sheets of paper at 2 units, pencils at 40 units and scissors at 100 units.

To start with, each group is given the quantities shown in the table below.

| Group | Paper | Pencils | Scissors | Rulers | Units of money |
|-------|-------|---------|----------|--------|----------------|
| A | 15 | 1 | 0 | 0 | 20 |
| B | 2 | 1 | 2 | 2 | 40 |
| C | 1 | 3 | 3 | 3 | 150 |
| D | 30 | 0 | 0 | 1 | 10 |
| E | 7 | 1 | 1 | 1 | 70 |
| F | 2 | 1 | 0 | 1 | 15 |

The groups can buy paper and machinery from each other at any rates that they can agree.

After about half an hour's work, stop the game. Ask each group to examine what it has in terms of money and resources. Compare these with the starting position. Who has done well? Why did they do better than the other groups?

The game is not meant to be fair, but it should show how some countries or groups can be exploited by others which have capital or technology. The discussion that follows the 'trading' period is the most important way of drawing out these points.

### Further activity
Share out a cake among the groups, with each slice corresponding in size to the 'wealth' of the group after the game. This can be a dramatic way of demonstrating the inequalities.

# 13. A safer workplace

### Foundation subject links
Technology, English.

### Age range
Five to nine (but would also work with older children).

### Group size
Four to six.

### What you need
Paper, pencils, pens, large sheets of paper, coloured pencils or paint and paintbrushes.

### What to do
Arrange to visit, as a group or as a class, a local workplace – the school kitchen would do. Ask the children to think about safety in the workplace. What rules do they have to follow in the classroom to keep safe? At home? On the street?

Before their visit, ask the children to predict what potential dangers there might be in the place that they are visiting. Make a list and ask them to suggest possible ways of avoiding them. This pre-visit activity will help observations become more focused when in the workplace.

At the workplace, encourage the children to ask the employees about safety rules and anything about their work considered dangerous. They might ask if there have been any accidents recently. Two useful people who might be interviewed would be the safety officer and a trade union representative.

Back in school, discuss with the class what they found out. Did their findings match their expectations? You could discuss the consequences of accidents, both for the individual and for the other people in the workplace. Who do the children think should be responsible for making sure the workplace is safe?

Ask the children if they could devise a set of safety rules for the workplace (or a better set than those currently used). Ask them to design posters publicising safety precautions. You could invite someone from the workplace to look at the posters or ask if they could be displayed there.

# 14. A better baked bean?

## Foundation subject links
Science, English, technology and geography.

## Age range
Five to eleven (in a modified form for the younger children).

## Group size
Four to six.

### What you need
A variety of brands of baked beans, clean plastic containers, water, spoons, small adhesive labels, paper, pencils, tea strainers, scales (optional).

### What to do
This activity is intended to generate a sense of consumer awareness. There are many different brands of baked beans, differently priced and with different qualities (or so the advertisements say!).

Begin with a discussion about the different manufacturers of baked beans: do the children know any brand names or own-label varieties? What are the differences? Do they or their parents have any preferences?

Ask the groups to examine the different tins. How much does each contain? What is the price? Older children could use calculators to work out the unit price. This is best expressed as the price per 100 grams (divide the price in pence by the net weight and multiply by 100).

What do the labels say the tins contain? The ingredients must be listed in order of weight, so compare the rank order of each tin. This could be in the form of a chart. What else do the labels say about the contents? Are particular varieties high in fibre or low in salt or sugar? If there is a low sugar content, do they contain artificial sweeteners?

When the children are not present, remove the label from each tin, and mark the tin and label it with an identifying number. Explain that this will allow the children to taste and test the beans 'blind', not knowing which bean is which. Discuss with them the qualities they could look for in beans. They might come up with a list that included such items as:
• appearance (no squashed beans, natural-looking colour);
• bean/sauce ratio (not too much of either);
• sweetness (not too sweet);

- other qualities of taste;
- how they feel in the mouth (not too hard, not too soft);
- aftertaste.

How can the children test these qualities? Use spoons to share out the beans into different containers (make sure that everything is labelled). Encourage the children to taste just a few beans of each variety (three or four should be enough) and then rinse out their mouths with sips of water between tastings. Discuss why these rules will help make the tests fairer. Make sure that they record their findings as they work. A scale of results will be more useful than just a tick or a cross.

If older children want to explore the bean/sauce ratio, they could use the tea strainers to filter off the beans and then weigh beans and sauce separately. It is more accurate if they weigh the initial contents, then rinse away the sauce under a tap, pat dry the beans on kitchen towelling and weigh the clean beans. The weight of sauce can then be calculated.

Make sure that all the children get an opportunity to examine and taste all the beans. Do their results agree? While they can discuss and perhaps agree on qualities such as colour and appearance, taste is more difficult to talk about.

Finally, reveal the brands of the beans they have been testing. Can they agree on the best-tasting beans? On the best-looking beans? On the cheapest? On what seems to be the healthiest?

## Further activity

If the children separate beans and sauce and rinse the sauce off the beans, do their taste ratings differ? How much of the overall taste is given by each of the two ingredients?

# 15. The old folks at home

## Foundation subject links
English, history, technology.

## Age range
Nine to eleven.

## Group size
Six to ten or the whole class.

## What you need
Everything necessary for a tea party – invitations, decorations, food and drink, teapots, cups, plates, cutlery, napkins, posters to advertise it.

## What to do
A group of children (perhaps the class) should form a mini-enterprise to provide a tea party for elderly people, possibly at a local day centre, or for local elderly people invited into the school. Giving is one way of exchanging goods and services – not all economic activities are based on buying and selling. The emphasis is on the children taking the initiative and making their own decisions as much as is possible.

The best baked beans....

They will need to discuss whom the party will be for and where it might be held. Having identified a group, they will need to find out what they would like to eat and drink. They might talk to some elderly people to find out. Perhaps it could be a 'theme' tea party, for example, the 1930s.

How will the children get the money they need to hold the party? How much will they need? Can they ask for contributions? From whom? Or should they organise some kind of sponsored event to raise funds?

Having collected the money, how will they organise the event? They must consider the date and time, planning and making any decorations, sending invitations. They must decide how they will prepare the food.

Many questions will arise at different points in the activity. Try to make the whole thing as realistic as possible and raise questions, rather than supply answers. The activity will spread over several days.

### Further activity
Ask the children to talk to their tea-party guests about life when they were young.

## 16. How did they get started?

### Foundation subject links
English, technology.

### Age range
Seven to eleven.

### Group size
Up to twelve.

### What you need
A friendly member of the local community who is prepared to talk quite freely with the children about financial matters; a tape recorder.

### What to do
How do businesses start? Very often a business starts with one person. He or she will save and borrow enough capital to start a small business based on a good idea, and then put in a great deal of work. Profits are saved and put back into expanding the business. Sometimes a business can be started by a group of people, perhaps working in a partnership or a co-operative.

Children can discover the realities and difficulties of starting a business by talking with people who have done this. Before they meet and talk to such a person, it will be useful to talk and discuss how they think businesses start: what is needed, who will have to do what, how long it might take and so on. Their ideas may be muddled and even apparently bizarre, but this process will allow them to form some hypotheses that they can test against what they discover in the ensuing interview.

Encourage the children to think of areas to discuss, rather than specific questions to ask. Either tape-record the interview or make detailed notes yourself (unless they are very used to doing this, note-taking will distract children from what is said). There are some more ideas on

developing interview techniques in Chapter 6 of *Inspirations for Speaking and Listening* by Alistair Ross (1992) Scholastic.

Try to get the business person to tell the children about his or her early efforts in some detail. How much money was needed and what was it for? What difficulties were there? Were there any disasters? Did the business expand?

After the interview, ask the children to discuss the stages that the person went through. They could create a chart or a strip cartoon to summarise the processes and the sequence involved.

# 17. Rules, rules, rules

## Foundation subject links
Technology, English.

## Age range
Seven to eleven; could be adapted for older infants.

## Group size
Groups of nine (modify the number of roles for smaller or larger groups).

## What you need
No specific requirements.

## What to do
This is a role-play activity that explores relationships at the workplace, especially rules and discipline.

Children in the group will take on different roles in a factory packaging sugar. Describe the process, eventually getting the children to mime the tasks. There is a huge hopper of sugar that empties sugar via an outlet gate into smaller containers, from which sugar is then scooped into bags, which are sealed, put into boxes and dispatched on a conveyor belt. Spilled sugar is swept up, put in another container and sent off as rubbish.

You should ask the children to play the following roles: one child to operate the hopper gate; two to put sugar in bags; two more to despatch boxes; one can be the supervisor; one child can have some responsibility for training, and another child can be the manager (away in the office). One of the workers is also the representative of the trade union. One child takes on the role of a new recruit.

The children should then enact the following scene: the supervisor asks the new recruit to sweep up spilled sugar and put it in the rubbish bin, but does not say which bin is which. The recruit puts the dirty sugar in one of the bins used for filling bags. It is not until several boxes of contaminated sugar have been sent off that the supervisor notices what has happened. The supervisor blames the recruit and sends for the manager to sack the recruit.

What happens? Who says what and to whom? What does the manager say to the supervisor and to the new worker? What does the supervisor say and do? What does the trade union representative say?

After all the views have been expressed (and perhaps a decision reached), ask the class to discuss the issues involved. What rights should workers have? How can businesses run smoothly and such rights be preserved?

### Further activity
Sometimes children develop stereotypes about trade union activity, for example, that the automatic response to any problem is to strike. One way of responding to this may be to ask a local trade union official to talk with the class (see Activity 19 on page 44).

# 18. What could you have done instead?

### Foundation subject links
English, mathematics.

### Age range
Five to eleven.

### Group size
Up to six.

### What you need
No specific requirements.

### What to do
'Opportunity cost' is a semi-technical term meaning what could have been done instead, if a particular course of action had not been taken. It is a way of assessing alternatives and choices, for example, spending

the day in a museum means that you cannot spend the same time on the beach. Ask the children in groups to discuss alternative ways of spending time and money.

With younger children, *Would you rather...* by John Burningham (Picture Lions) would be an appropriate starting point. It offers a series of choices (most of them rather unpleasant fantasies) and asks children which they would rather do. This creates an opportunity to discuss the alternatives, in this case, which is the least worst scenario.

Older children might consider different ways of spending the day on a school outing. Given that there is only one day, of a fixed duration, what can be fitted in and what does this 'cost' in terms of leaving things out? Will fitting everything in satisfy anyone?

The children might discuss alternative activities they could organise at the school fair. Which activities would raise the most money? Should they spend all their time and energy organising and running these or are there other, less remunerative activities which add to the fun of the fair?

They might also discuss alternative ways of spending pocket money. Buying one thing means that something else cannot be bought. What criteria are used in judging alternatives?

## 19. Union

### Foundation subject links
English.

### Age range
Nine to eleven.

### Group size
The whole class, divided into two groups if this makes discussion easier to organise.

### What you need
A trade union official (a shop steward or local organiser). Your local Trades Council may be able to help find someone.

### What to do
Invite a trade union official to talk with the children about her work. It is not always easy to arrange such talks, because union representatives are often busy, and if she is an unpaid official, she may not easily get time off work to visit a school.

Ask the trade union official to talk about specific and recent instances of the union activities, for example, claims for industrial injuries, negotiating wage rises or participation in health and safety exercises. Encourage the children to ask questions. To make the most of this opportunity the children should discuss the issues they wish to raise beforehand, to form some preconceptions about the role of a union worker, which they can then compare with the activities described in the interview.

If you are concerned about appearing politically biased in organising such an activity, the interview could be linked to Activity 16 (see page 41), which should ensure a balance of viewpoints.

### Further activity
Take the children to visit the union official at her place of work.

## 20. Paying for pollution

### Foundation subject links
Science, technology.

### Age range
Seven to eleven.

### Group size
The whole class, dividing into smaller groups where appropriate.

### What you need
Access to the personnel of the local cleansing department.

### What to do
Visit the local council's cleansing department. Ask the children to find out what the work involves and speak with managers about how much it costs to run the collection system.

What happens to the waste that is collected? How is it sorted? Why? What items can be recycled? What sort of market is there for recyclable materials?

Some local authorities have extensive recycling schemes that involve householders in sorting out domestic rubbish into different containers for collection. Others have bottle and aluminium banks at central points. Some councils even supply containers with worms and microbes to digest organic rubbish into garden compost!

Ask the class to investigate the alternatives, with an emphasis on cost and value for money. Who should pay for generating rubbish? Who should be responsible – the

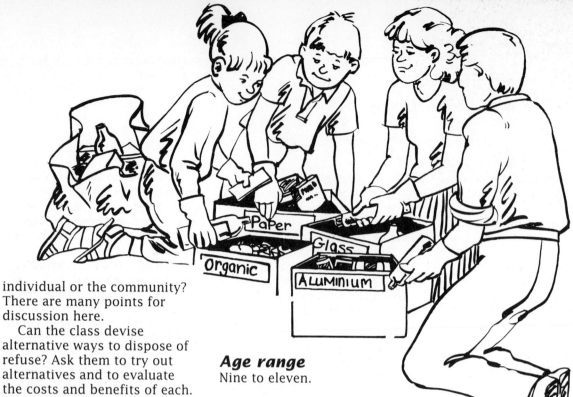

individual or the community? There are many points for discussion here.

Can the class devise alternative ways to dispose of refuse? Ask them to try out alternatives and to evaluate the costs and benefits of each. Take the best solutions to the local council or invite the cleansing department manager into school to see the proposals and to discuss them with the class.

### Further activity

Ask the class to consider other examples of pollution and ask them who they think should pay for dealing with them. Acid rain from burning fossil fuels may cause damage hundreds of miles away from the source of pollution. Who can tell who is responsible? Global warming is caused by hundreds of millions of individual decisions: who can regulate this and make the polluter pay?

## 21. Open all hours

### Foundation subject links

English, mathematics, technology.

### Age range

Nine to eleven.

### Group size

The whole class, divided into groups of two and three.

### What you need

Clipboards, photocopiable pages 170 and 171 (or devise your own), pencils.

### What to do

When should different kinds of shops be open? What do shopkeepers think? What about customers? This activity asks children to conduct two surveys into opinion – that of the general public and that of shopkeepers.

Begin with a class discussion about shopping hours and times. What days and hours do different shops open? What hours would be convenient for different people? How do they think shop workers feel about it? The children can either use the questionnaires on photocopiable pages 170 and 171 or devise their own.

Ask the children to use one set of questionnaires with the general public and with parents. You might discuss with them if they are likely to get different kinds of results from talking to people on the street at, say, 10.30am than they would at 6.30pm. Why is this?

The children should use the second set to interview people working in shops. Do the children think that people who work in shops and shop owners might give different answers?

Ask the class to compare the results of the two surveys. They could construct bar charts and graphs, or make a map of the local area to show late shopping. If possible, encourage the children to use a computer data-handling program to analyse the results more quickly and thoroughly.

### Further activity

Ask the class to publish a report of their findings for parents and visitors to the school.

# CHAPTER 2

# Health education

The inclusion of health education as a cross-curricular theme is not controversial. Teachers and parents have generally accepted that school has an important part to play in raising children's understanding and awareness of how they should live in a healthy way. Children need knowledge about how their bodies and minds work; they need to develop attitudes that encourage taking care of themselves, and they need experience of taking responsibility and making decisions (based on their knowledge) that allow them to meet their needs.

Health education is, therefore, more than simply a collection of biological facts. It is concerned with using scientific information to take preventive action and doing so on a variety of levels. While any society might have some specialists in this area, who have particular skills and powers to take action for the whole community (for example, environmental health officers), they cannot advise on or control all the everyday activities of individuals. Responsibility for individual health care lies, for very young children, with the family, and very soon in life, with the individual child and the adult. Learning how to care for oneself (simple hygiene, eating sensibly, taking sufficient exercise, avoiding accidents) are some of children's earliest learning experiences. Responsibility and supervision may lie with adults, but many of these activities are among the first major responsibilities to be shifted towards the developing child.

Health education is thus of particular importance in primary education. Attitudes towards self-responsibility are developed in these years, and these will affect the responses of young people towards health hazards and health-related activities later in life.

It is for these reasons that health education is necessarily identified as a cross-curricular theme; it is not of the same character and nature as an aspect of science. Scientific knowledge is applied, but in a context of personal and social development, using a whole range of skills and knowledge from across the curriculum, synthesised to form particular attitudes towards taking care of oneself.

### Changes in health care

The responsibility for health care is shared between community, groups and individuals. There was a time in Britain when the state took on very little responsibility for health care, which rested with the individual or the family, and sometimes with local and voluntary groups. But as the treatment of disease and of health-related problems became more specialised and expensive, concern focused on treatment and cure, rather than prevention. 'Getting ill' and 'going to the doctor or hospital' were activities which worried the population much more than they do now because they involved unforeseen, unpredictable and uncontrollable expense. The maintenance of health was (understandably) eclipsed in peoples' consciousness by the treatment of illness.

By the time of the development of a publicly-financed health service, this attention on the cure, rather than on prevention, had become dominant. Many of the founders of the National Health Service believed that after an initial rush of patients, the backlog of disease would be dealt with and that the new system would be largely dealing with emergencies and with long-term prevention. But the extent of ill-health had been underestimated, and was only revealed as more and more people came forward for treatment. The treatment of disease quickly dominated the agenda of the health service, with comparatively few resources, energy or attention being given to prevention. Some research suggests that as health care services expand, people are more likely to declare themselves ill. This is not to suggest that such people are malingerers or hypochondriacs, but that the state of 'being ill' is fluid and

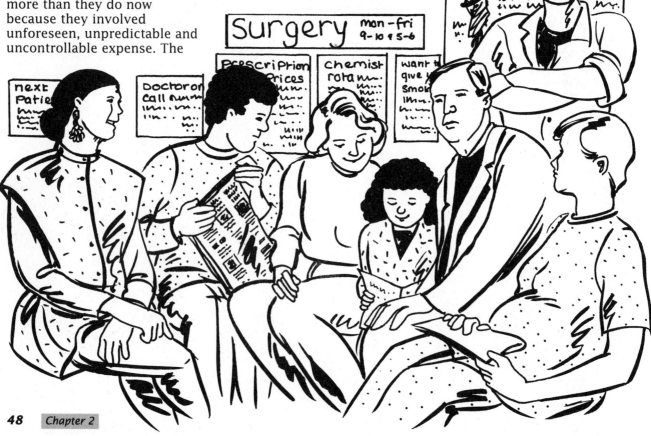

that conditions which people used to put up with are now perceived as treatable.

The greater emphasis on health education which has developed over the past twenty years has, in part, been the result of the recognition that demand for treatment is continuing to rise, and, in part, because more preventable health problems are arising. Prevention is not only better than cure; it is also likely to be cheaper and to lead ultimately to fewer demands on hard-pressed health professionals. Of course, not all ill-health is preventable.

## A matter of major concern

The major advances in public health in the past, undertaken by communities, national governments and international agencies, have cut dramatically many of the infectious and water-borne diseases. Smallpox has been eradicated; diseases such as measles and tuberculosis are now minimal in the developed world, and moving towards a state of control elsewhere. This leaves other preventable illnesses in a more prominent position. With the elimination of many of the fatal childhood diseases in Britain over the past years, we now have a situation where accidents are the most common form of death for the under thirties. The effects of environmental pressures, of dietary factors and of social behaviour all contribute greatly towards the present-day incidence of ill-health and premature death.

For example, heart diseases and strokes are related closely to diet, smoking, and lack of exercise. Some 38 per cent of all deaths in the UK are a result of heart disease and strokes; nearly nine per cent of NHS costs are in treating these, and 43 million working days are lost each year as a consequence. Although heart

disease and smoking are rare among young children, the behaviour that leads to them is often fixed by the age of eleven. Analysis of ten-year-olds' blood cholesterol levels shows patterns that can be used to predict accurately future heart disease, and by the age of 20, there is often quite a lot of arterial damage. These levels of damage can be directly related to children's dietary habits. For many people, smoking begins before they become teenagers. Exercise habits are also becoming established before children reach secondary school. So, although such major causes of death are not obviously of relevance to children (or their parents and teachers), there is a great deal that primary children can learn and do that will lead to future health.

Cancers account for 25 per cent of deaths and many of these seem to be attributable to environmental conditions. Smoking leads to about a third of these deaths.

Current government policy is to target five key areas of action and to identify four risk factors. Targets have been set to reduce the incidence of:
• heart disease and strokes,
• cancers,
• mental illness,
• sexual ill-health,
• accidents.

The risk factors are:
• smoking,
• diet and nutrition,
• blood pressure,
• HIV/Aids.
(*Health of the Nation* [HMSO] 1992)

The response to health education has to be more individualistic in the future. This is not a matter of political philosophy, but the consequence of the changes in health standards that have taken place in the recent past. Many of the areas in which community or national policy has operated in the past have succeeded. Disease rates have tumbled. There is still plenty of room for governmental action, but many of the health problem areas that are left are ones for which the individual must have prime responsibility – questions of diet, exercise, smoking and other drug use, sexually-transmitted diseases and so on. In any society, other than the most rigorously controlled, these are matters on which individuals must make decisions for themselves. Clearly, the

community and the government can help (for example, in controlling environmental health hazards or in medical research and provision), but in terms of avoidance it has to be the individual who understands and takes active steps to avoid dangers to health.

## Children's ideas about health

Children have their own ideas about health. Most children put together a series of imperfect models of how their bodies function and use this to justify (or evade) the various health advice that they are given. Dietary information, for example, is frequently used to create blanket categories of 'good' and 'bad' food, often with little regard for the actual constituents of the food in question. This sometimes works on a form of association or similarity, for example, because cooked white fish is thought to resemble brain tissue, fish is thought to be 'good' food for the brain. Similarly, red meat may be believed to increase and strengthen muscles.

Similar misconceptions sometimes apply in the understanding of the dangers of smoking. 'If you don't inhale it's quite safe', or 'only puff the first half and then throw the rest away' are two common beliefs, often passed on by older children.

As a first step in raising any topic in health education, it can be extremely useful for the teacher to discuss with the children their own questions and the possible solutions. This will help you to determine the children's own starting points, and to identify the kinds of information and approaches that will be the most fruitful to explore. You will also find out about any underlying misconceptions that need to be untangled and, if necessary, demolished before moving forward. Without having any model of the child's existing framework, it is quite possible for the children to try to fit new information from you into the set of misleading beliefs that they already hold.

## The role of the school

Shocking or frightening children about health care issues rarely works – it is also ineffective with adults. Simply providing information is also insufficient. Children either disregard the information or discount it in some way, for example, by acknowledging the risk but suggesting that it will not happen to them. In order to develop a proper sense of awareness and a willingness to take informed decisions, teaching strategies are needed that allow the class or a group to assess

information, to negotiate with others, to listen carefully to each other, and to make and deal with relationships. As suggested in the introduction to this book, active learning is essential: games, simulations, role-playing, problem-solving exercises, actively gathering information through questionnaires and surveys. All these are likely to be more effective than direct teaching and over-reliance on visual aids.

Many issues raised under the umbrella of health education are sensitive matters. This needs to be carefully handled by the teacher, so that individuals are not unduly embarrassed and personal matters are not inadvertently disclosed. It is possible for children themselves to establish a set of rules for discussion that

minimise personal distress. In the National Curriculum Council booklet *Curriculum Guidance 5* (1990), one set of eleven-year-olds have been cited who came up with the following ground rules:
• Listen to what other people say.
• Don't be nasty to each other.
• No talking when someone else is talking.
• Be kind to each other and give support.
• If all you can say is something unpleasant, don't say anything at all.
• If people don't want to say anything, they don't have to.
• Don't laugh at what other people say.
• Think before you ask a question.

### The major areas covered by health education

The National Curriculum Council's document *Health Education* (1990) suggests nine components to the health

education curriculum. All of these are necessary areas for all ages of children, although clearly different approaches will be needed with different age groups, as children and young people become increasingly responsible for different aspects of their behaviour.

## Substance abuse and misuse

Tobacco consumption among young people remains disturbingly high and although it affects only a minority of primary children, an attitude against the possibility of smoking can be encouraged and developed. The same is true of alcohol use. Frightening children about the consequences does not seem to work. It is difficult to see dangers in something that adults legally do that does not always lead to death or illness, and if it does so, it is only after a long period of time.

'If it was really dangerous, the government would ban it,' said one nine-year-old, with a touching belief in the power of logic. Unfortunately, the evidence seems to show that banned substances enjoy at least some of their popularity with young people precisely because they are illicit.

Infant children need to understand the complicated way in which we use the words 'drug' and 'medicine'. All medicines are drugs, but not all drugs are medicines (see Figure 1 below). They need to know a little about the different kinds of medicines and how some people need regular medication in order to lead a normal life. Virtually any substance can be misused and be harmful to people, so the children must also understand safety rules about the need for adult help in taking medicines, treating household cleaners and other substances with care and so on.

Junior children will also need to know about how some medicines can be bought freely and others need to be prescribed, and why; and that some substances are illegal. They will need to develop techniques of resisting pressure from friends and learning to say 'no'. They should also be aware of the enormous benefits that some drugs have brought to people.

## Sex education

This area of the curriculum is particularly governed by law. The 1986 Education Act (No 2) requires the school's governing body '...to consider separately [...] the question whether sex education should

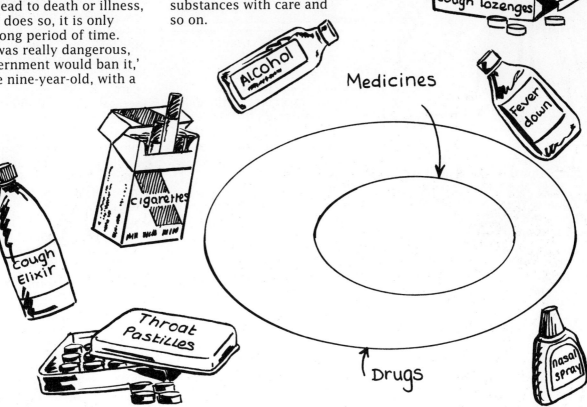

Figure 1

form part of the secular curriculum for the school; and to make and keep up to date, a separate written statement of their policy with regard to the content and organisation of the relevant part of the curriculum; or, where they conclude that sex education should not form part of the secular curriculum, of that conclusion.'

Most governing bodies seem to have decided that sex education will be included in their curriculum, but some have made particular requirements for consultation with parents before such

teaching takes place. This latter policy makes it difficult for sex education to take place outside a strictly-defined slot. However, the governors have absolute discretion in this matter.

Sex education will take place irrespective of any input by the teacher. It is important that it does occur in the primary school, not least because some ten per cent of the Year 6 girls will reach puberty before they leave, and they have the right to know what is happening to their bodies. A recent survey found that just under a fifth of girls of this age were totally unprepared and that very few primary schools had adequate lavatory provision for these girls, or for the disposal of

sanitary towels. However, it is not just these girls who need to be prepared for the physical, emotional and social changes that are beginning to take place in the upper junior years. Children will increasingly need to be aware of sexual relationships, of what kinds of touching of their bodies are improper and should be resisted, and of sexually-transmitted diseases. Three quarters of eleven-year-olds know how HIV is transmitted and a third know that condoms can be used to prevent transmission. At the age of eleven, children appear to be very sympathetic to the idea of supporting friends and others who may be HIV-positive, but by the age of thirteen, much of this feeling of support seems to have evaporated (*Who's Telling the Children?* Barnardos, 1992).

The National Curriculum Council suggest that infant children need to be able to name female and male reproductive parts of the body, and understand the idea of male and female. It is essential for children to recognise that they as individuals have rights over their own bodies, and that there is a difference between good and bad touching. They must realise that they can say 'no' and that they should tell a sympathetic adult if they feel they are being touched improperly or otherwise abused. They should also know about the special needs of babies and appreciate how human beings develop.

Junior children should have some understanding of the changes that come at puberty. This will include the basic biological aspects of human reproduction, an understanding of basic parenting skills and different patterns of friendship.

### Family life education

The National Curriculum Council's statement on 'family life education' describes its objectives in the following terms:

'The principal objective of family life education is that pupils understand and value the central role of the family as an institution and the important part it plays in the development of attachment, love and concern.'

This ignores the possibility that 'attachment, love and concern' can exist in relationships other than the family and that children can develop quite satisfactorily in such situations. It may also make it a difficult area for discussion when there are children in the class who have a home relationship that is not of the conventional 'family' type.

It is, however, possible to interpret 'family' in a wider sense, to include a number of types of relationships within the home; this would allow the teacher to include single-parent families, foster families and other relationships within the broad definition.

Infant children should know of the variety of families, of the rituals associated with family events such as birth,

marriage and death, and know how people grow from babyhood to old age.

Junior children should know more about the stages of human development, particularly about patterns of child-rearing and about the needs of the elderly and the infirm. They should know about agencies which support families and individuals in various difficult circumstances.

### Safety

Now that most childhood diseases that were formerly dangerous are no longer fatal, accidents are the major cause of death in children of school age. Safety education teaches children how to respond in a variety of environments and encourages them to develop strategies and skills to keep themselves and others safe.

With infants, this will mean knowing about the potential dangers in the local environment, for example, on the road, near water and in the home. An awareness of the hazards will be a necessary precursor to developing strategies of avoidance that will come later. Keeping safe will entail avoiding danger and knowing how to find help if danger occurs.

By the time children are of junior age they should be using simple safety procedures in, for example, crossing the road or in knowing and following rules for using particular tools in design and technology work. They should be accepting some responsibilities for their own and others' safety. They should also know some simple first aid measures, for example, the need to wash cuts and keep them clean.

### Health-related exercise

Regular exercise can play an important part in both promoting and maintaining health. It is establishing the link between exercise and

health that is important, so that children find reasons to persist with it.

Infant children need to know that people feel better when they take regular exercise. This can mean asking them to consider how they feel after physical activities, for example, concentrating on the positive feelings expressed. They also need to understand that when they exercise, they are using up some of their energy, and that this energy is replaced by eating food.

Junior children will have a more sophisticated understanding of the role of exercise, knowing, for example, that it strengthens bones, muscles and organs such as the heart, and keeps their bodies agile and supple. They should also be aware of the balance between food intake and the use of energy, realising that if their intake of energy through food exceeds their energy use, their bodies will begin to store the excess as fat.

### Food and nutrition

The relationship between diet and health is complex, covering both the range of types of food and the quantities involved. Children are increasingly subjected to commercial pressures on their eating habits, and they need to develop a healthy scepticism about the motives of food manufacturers and food outlets. The relationship between energy use and energy intake is important in considering the need for changes in dietary habits, and while children need to recognise the wide range of healthy bodily shapes, they also need to be aware of the choices and control that they have in eating, so that the dangers of both overeating and undereating are avoided.

This area is also concerned with the different nutritional qualities of different foodstuffs. Children need to develop an understanding of the major types of nutrients, what part each plays in maintaining bodily health and functions and the balance that needs to be achieved. Much of the emphasis should be on helping children realise the personal choice and control

that they have. However, there should also be the opportunity to understand the role that the government could play in setting or changing standards in food processing (for example, to cut levels of saturates, sugar or sodium), or the way in which farming can be influenced to produce more high-fibre products.

Infant children should be developing an awareness of the wide range of foodstuffs that they can choose from. This choice is determined by availability, needs, cultural preferences and prohibitions, and economic factors. They should also know that food is needed for health and for energy, and that some foods are better than others for these purposes.

Junior children should be able to analyse diet as a combination of foodstuffs, and to recognise the different nutrients in some of these. They should know how various nutrients (such as carbohydrates, fats, proteins and vitamins) have different effects and uses in their bodies. The balance that they achieve through their diet can influence their health negatively, as well as positively. They should know how to handle foods safely. They should be aware of the importance of additives in keeping food safe and of some of the concerns about them.

### Personal hygiene

An important aspect of health maintenance is keeping clean. Developing a sense of pride in one's body and consequently maintaining it in good condition leads to habits of good personal hygiene. This is also related to knowledge of the variety of infectious diseases that can be transmitted if personal hygiene is not maintained.

Infant children should learn the need for simple personal health routines such as washing their hands, cleaning their teeth and blowing their noses. As part of this, they will begin to understand that some diseases can be transmitted if such routines are not followed.

Junior children will be increasingly responsible for aspects of their personal cleanliness. They will know, for example, about dental decay and practising good dental hygiene. Older juniors will also need to be prepared for the changes of puberty and how these will affect personal hygiene.

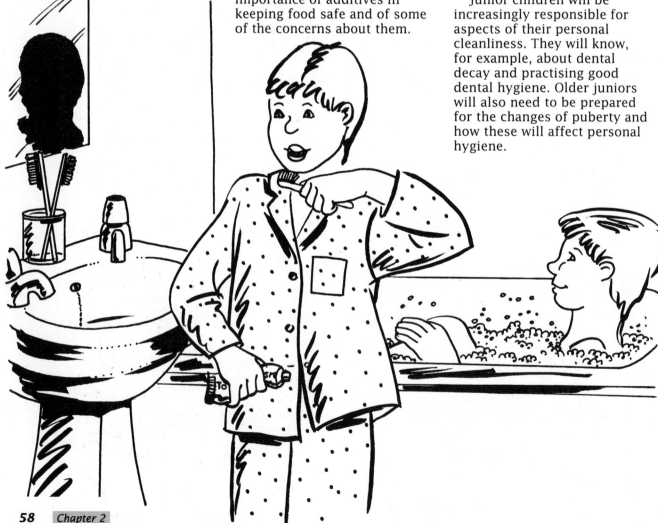

## Environmental aspects of health education

Many environmental health hazards lie outside the control of most individuals, but some are avoidable. Health education therefore involves both developing an awareness of how the environment can influence health and illness, and how social and community pressure can be used to influence the producers of environmental hazards where avoidance is not possible, or not enough. There are a variety of social, physical and economic factors at play in determining the nature and extent of environmental health hazards, and the interrelationships between these need to be appreciated.

Infants should be beginning to understand the part that people play in a range of environments (for example, home, school, workplaces and shops, country and town areas) and that people have a responsibility of caring for their environment. Rules are made to help individuals care in this way.

Juniors should be aware of the variety of values and attitudes that affect people's behaviour towards the environment. They should also know about environmental hazards and be able to make suggestions about how to avoid them, for example, leaded petrol.

## Psychological aspects of health education

Health is in part a psychological state or a frame of mind. People who have a degree of tolerance, who are prepared to accept a range of behaviours and emotional responses, are likely to be healthier and more balanced in their outlook than those who expect everyone else to conform to their own notions of correctness. This aspect of health education is therefore concerned with developing states of emotional well-being which minimise stress and maximise self-awareness.

Infant children should understand why it is important to value both themselves and others, and how people feel and behave if they are not valued. They should be aware of some of the range of emotions that they and others show, and how to deal with these positively.

Junior children should understand that individuals may have different roles in the groups to which they belong. They should recognise individuality in this way, and also in the way that people respond emotionally to various events. They should understand loyalty and friendships, and develop the range of skills needed to develop and maintain relationships.

# ACTIVITIES

## 1. Exercise measures

### Foundation subject links
Science, mathematics and technology.

### Age range
Five to eleven, with appropriate adaptations.

### Group size
Pairs or groups of four.

### What you need
Watches with second hands, paper, pencils.

### What to do
Ask the children what happens when they do physical activities. They may reply that they feel hot, sweaty or that they start to pant. Explain that they are going to investigate how their bodies change when they start to exercise.

**NB:** All children doing this activity must be physically fit. No child who is excused games or PE activities on medical grounds should be allowed to carry out this activity.

Two fairly simple items to measure are the heart rate and the respiration rate (breathing). Ask the children to find and measure their pulse (easiest in the wrist – on the palm side next to the thumb – or at the temple). This can be difficult as some children just count numbers instead of counting what they feel!

Ask the children to work in pairs. They should first measure their heart rate (the number of beats in 60 seconds) when they are at rest. It can help if they lie still for five minutes beforehand. Then ask them to take vigorous exercise for two minutes: climbing on to a chair and down again as fast as possible is pretty vigorous. Ask them to measure the heart rate again as soon as the two minutes are up. They could make a third set of measurements two minutes later.

Why does the heart rate increase? It does so partly to increase the supply of blood to the muscles – taking to them sugars and oxygen, and removing from them the breakdown products or releasing the energy. The increased blood flow also helps transmit heat to the skin, where it can be lost through sweating.

How fast does the heart rate return to normal? One of the signs of good health is when the heart rate quickly returns to its original resting pace. If children take regular strong exercise their recovery rate should decrease.

Ask the children to measure their respiratory rate in the same way. One breath is an inhalation and an exhalation. Ask them to think about why the breathing rate might change. Does it recover as quickly as the heart rate?

### Further activity
Ask the children to devise an instrument to measure the heart rate or the breathing rate more accurately – perhaps some mechanism to magnify the movement of the pulse, so it can be seen more easily.

# 2. Now wash your hands!

## Foundation subject links
Science, technology.

## Age range
Five to nine.

## Group size
Groups of three to five and some whole-class discussion.

## What you need
Access to a washbasin, aprons, soap, paper towels, some strong washable non-toxic colouring matter, preferably a dark colour (powdered paint will do).

## What to do
Microbes are so small that they are invisible. It is relatively easy to wash away visible dirt – at least one can see a surface that appears to be clean. However, invisible microbes are harder to deal with.

Explain to the children that the paint or dyestuff represents the microbes. Ask them to put on the aprons. Put some paint on one child's hand and send him to wash his hands clean. As he turns on the water, he will contaminate the tap. He must then scrub his hands clean, but when he turns the water off, he re-contaminates his hands. The next child who uses the basin will suffer the same fate.

Activities such as this one demonstrate how easy it is to transfer microbes from person to person and how even scrubbing hands clean may not solve the problem. Ask the children to come up with suggestions for improving washing arrangements, so that hand-washing does not necessarily lead to re-contamination.

## Further activity
Try similar experiments to see if hand towels can pass on infections. This could be linked to work in the area of economic and industrial understanding, on the relative costs of hand towels and hot-air hand driers.

# 3. Temper, temper!

## Foundation subject links
English, science.

## Age range
Seven to nine.

## Group size
Pairs, with perhaps a class discussion afterwards.

## What you need
No special requirements.

## What to do
Role-play an incident in which one person loses her temper with the other, perhaps through a misunderstanding. It is best to give the children a few rules before they start: no touching, no shouting and to stop role-play as soon as they are told. The task of the second person is to try to calm down the first person. What sort of things does he say? How does the other person respond?

After the role-play, ask the children to discuss how and why they lose their temper. What sort of things make them angry? How do they calm down? What effect does their loss of temper have on other people?

## Further activity
Use similar techniques to explore other emotions such as fear and fright.

# 4. Saying 'no'

### Foundation subject links
Science, English.

### Age range
Seven to eleven.

### Group size
Four to six.

### What you need
No special requirements.

### What to do
One of the main reasons why young people start using cigarettes (or taking illegal drugs) is peer pressure. This role-play is designed to help children develop strategies to resist this, empowering them to say 'no'. Explain this to the group beforehand.

Ask one child to be the non-smoker, whom the others are going to try to persuade to start smoking. What do the 'smokers' say? Make notes of the different techniques they try – flattery, mockery, accusations, reasoned arguments. How does the 'victim' respond?

Try the role-play again with two non-smokers. Is it easier for them to support each other?

Discuss the kinds of pressure that are being used. How good are the 'smokers' at putting forward their arguments?

### Further activity
Reverse the activity: ask a group of non-smokers to try to persuade a pretend 'smoker' to give up.

# 5. Good drugs, bad drugs

### Foundation subject links
Science.

### Age range
Seven to eleven.

### Group size
Five to eight.

## What you need

A set of cards, each with the name of a drug or other substance written on it. The list on photocopiable page 172 could be used to make the cards.

## What to do

Discuss what the words 'drug' and 'medicine' mean. A drug is a substance that has an effect – good or bad – on the way in which the body operates. 'Drug' is also often used to mean an addictive substance or one that causes damage. Explain that medicines are a particular category of the term 'drug'.

Each set of cards should contain some medical drugs, some dangerous drugs and some things that may or may not be drugs, and may or may not be dangerous. Ask the children to discuss the cards and sort them into categories. Some of the cards will pose

difficulties. Are vitamins drugs? If so, can cornflakes be drugs? What about cough pastilles?

The aim of this activity is to stimulate discussion and to recognise that some of the categories may not be easy to define. The alcohol in the whisky can be a drug and can be dangerous, but is sometimes regarded as medicinal and a prescription is not necessary. Try to encourage these sorts of discussions and let the children create their own categories. You could point out that opium and cocaine used to be freely available in this country. Under very specific circumstances they are still used as medicines today, but only in special cases, and only on a doctor's prescription.

After the different groups have come to their conclusions, ask the class to share the results and to justify their categories. Discuss with the children what their attitude should be towards these substances. Which would they be able to use on their own? Which would need parental supervision? Which drugs are dangerous?

## Further activity

The children could devise posters about safety with medicines or about drug abuse.

## Further activities

Ask the children to write decorated thank-you notes to the people they talked to. Visit or invite them again and find out more about their lives and the changes they have seen.

# 7. Medicine labels

### Foundation subject links
Science, technology.

### Age range
Seven to eleven.

### Group size
Individuals, pairs or small groups.

### What you need
Some empty medicine containers, with their labels still on; paper, felt-tipped pens, paints.

### What to do
Ask the class to discuss the sort of information that a medicine container should have on its label.

Ask the children to look at some containers and see what sort of information is given. Discuss how useful this is. Could it be explained better? What sort of warnings or advice should be given? How is this best done?

Ask the children to design some medicine container labels. How will it be made clear that medicines should only be taken by the person for whom they were prescribed and only in the quantities indicated?

The children could design some posters on the safe use of medicines. The best posters could then be displayed around the school.

# 6. Growing old

### Foundation subject links
Science, history, English.

### Age range
Five to eleven.

### Group size
Small groups or the whole class.

### What you need
Some elderly people prepared to talk with the children, who could either come to the school or be visited at, for example, a day centre; thin card, coloured pencils, scissors, felt-tipped pens.

### What to do
Ageing involves a variety of changes to the body and mind. Ask the class to think about some of the changes that affect people as they age, in terms of, for example, mobility, balance, eating, memory and physical appearance.

Ask the children to talk with some elderly people about when they were young and the changes that they have seen. From this, they might go on to talk about changes in their lives, and things that they can now do that they could not do when they were younger, and vice versa.

While ageing is usually thought of negatively, it is also possible to see positive aspects: old people travel more now than they used to, for example. Very few will have flown between continents in their youth. They also have much more to remember and reminisce about than young people.

After the event, encourage the children to exchange information about the different aspects of ageing that they noticed.

# 8. Plaque marks

### Foundation subject links
Science, technology.

### Age range
Seven to nine, but also possible with both younger and older children.

### Group size
Pairs.

### What you need
Ask the children to bring their toothbrushes and toothpaste to school in a plastic bag with their name on it; you will also need disclosing tablets (from the chemist) and small mirrors.

### What to do
Talk about dental care. You may be able to involve the school nurse in this activity.

Explain that disclosing tablets are designed to stain temporarily the invisible build-up of plaque that forms on teeth. They show exactly how well teeth are being cleaned and the bits that get missed, by staining the plaque a bright-red colour, so it can be easily seen (and then attacked with a toothbrush).

Either ask the children to clean their teeth first and then use the disclosing tablets immediately afterwards to show how effective their cleaning has been; or, alternatively, use the tablets straight away (perhaps immediately after lunch) and go on to tooth-cleaning after this.

Ask the school nurse or dentist to demonstrate the best ways to brush teeth or do this yourself. Use up-and-down movements to dislodge plaque and particles and cover all the surfaces of the teeth.

You could talk with the children about how dental care has improved over the past decades. Nowadays most young people should expect, if they clean their teeth and visit the dentist regularly, to keep most of their teeth into old age. In the 1940s, most people over fifty had lost nearly all their teeth and quite a lot of twenty-year-olds had only false teeth.

### Further activity
Ask the children to make posters on dental care.

# 9. Rotting teeth

### Foundation subject links
Science.

### Age range
Five to eleven.

### Group size
Any size.

### What you need
A few teeth, glass jars with screw-top lids, fizzy drinks, chocolate, various types of sweets.

### What to do
Persuade some children to let you have some of their milk teeth that have come out. Ask the children to clean the teeth and then put them into glass jars with screw tops. Add various substances to each: fizzy drinks, chocolate (with water), boiled sweets (with water) and other sweets (with water).

Seal the bottles and set them aside for several weeks. Re-examine the bottles carefully to check the effect of the drinks and sweets. This can be a dramatic and effective way of curtailing sweet consumption!

Ask the class to look at other factors contributing to tooth decay.

# 10. Road safety

## Foundation subject links
Technology, English.

## Age range
Five to eleven.

## Group size
Four to eight for group work; some whole-class activities.

## What you need
Paper, pencils, clipboards, materials for posters.

## What to do
Take the children for a walk in the local area to look at how safety is maintained on and around the roads. Ask them to examine:
• pedestrian crossings and the road markings around them;
• street signs, with older children distinguishing signs that instruct (circles) from signs that warn (triangles) and signs that inform (rectangles);
• ways in which traffic is regulated;
• provisions for pedestrians, cyclists and people with disabilities.

They should look particularly at how people behave in order to stay safe.

Do pedestrians look around themselves properly before crossing the roads? Do they wait for the 'cross now' signs? Do motorists cross on amber or red lights? Do cyclists obey traffic lights? Do cars stop at pedestrian crossings if someone is waiting to cross?

Discuss the findings with the children. Many adults take shortcuts with the traffic safety rules. Is this advisable? Is it safe?

Ask the children, working in groups, to devise road safety rules that make it clear what pedestrians should do to keep safe. They could devise posters that explain the importance of following safety rules.

## Further activity
Invite the local road safety officer to school to look at and comment on the posters.

# 11. Water safety

### Foundation subject links
PE, design, English.

### Age range
Five to eleven.

### Group size
Pairs and the whole class.

### What you need
Materials to make posters.

### What to do
Visit a local place where there is water such as a swimming pool, a canal, a river or a beach. Ask the children to identify possible dangers and to look for any warnings, signs or indications of how dangers might be dealt with. Discuss aspects of safety with any people who are responsible for safety at the site (for example, a swimming pool attendant, a coastguard).

In class, ask the children to identify the hazards and to discuss the dangers that are possible in the water. Identify with them all the activities that are dangerous and all the safety precautions that should be taken. Discuss ways of making these widely known and understood.

Ask the children to make posters that highlight the safety rules. They could think of slogans that will make the message memorable.

### Further activity
Devise an assembly for the whole school to bring home the points about water safety.

# 12. Family trees

### Foundation subject links
English, history.

### Age range
Seven to eleven.

### Group size
Individuals and small groups.

### What you need
Paper, felt-tipped pens, rulers, card, thread, garden cane, scissors.

### What to do
Discuss different kinds of families: large ones, small ones, ones with one parent and those with two. Include references to adoption, divorce and separation, death and bereavement, living with people, marriage and remarriage, so that all children in the class feel that their family circumstances are discussable and not seen in any way as abnormal or incorrect. Types of family structures are much less sensitive than they used to be, but it is important that all children feel that judgements are not being made on them or their families by the teacher, the school or other children in the class.

Discuss how the definition of a family can vary: it can mean simply those living in the same home, the strict biological nuclear family or the extended family. Children's definitions will vary according to context and culture.

Draw a family tree for the class. It could be your own. Show how different generations are shown on different horizontal levels, how children are shown in relation to their parents and so on.

Ask the children to draw their own family trees or the family tree of an imaginary family. This allows children the option of disclosing their own details or not, as they choose. Encourage those drawing their own trees to find out more about other members of their family whom they might include, perhaps their great-grandparents.

### Further activity
The children could make the family trees into mobiles, with cut-out figures hanging from threads tied to pieces of garden cane.

# 13. Babies and their needs

## Foundation subject links
Science, English.

## Age range
Five to nine.

## Group size
Three to four.

## What you need
A mother with a young baby, prepared to visit the class.

## What to do
Ask the mother to talk with the children about looking after the baby. While it is best to do this in small groups, it will be hard to achieve this as the whole class will want to watch and help at nappy-changing time, or feeding time!

If possible, arrange for the baby to be bathed in class. Some mothers may be happy to show children how to hold the baby safely.

Discuss with the children how babies need things done for them and how they are learning to do some things for themselves. Can the children remember when they were very young? They could also ask their parents what they could do when they were toddlers or babies.

## Further activity
It would be ideal if the same baby could be brought back to visit the class on four or five occasions over the year. Take photographs and encourage the children to write down what the baby can do at each stage.

# 14. Dealing with stress

## Foundation subject links
English, geography.

## Age range
Five to eleven.

## Group size
Small groups, covering the whole class eventually.

## What you need
No special requirements.

## What to do
Some children may be subjected to enormous amounts of stress at times. This may be caused by such things as homelessness or

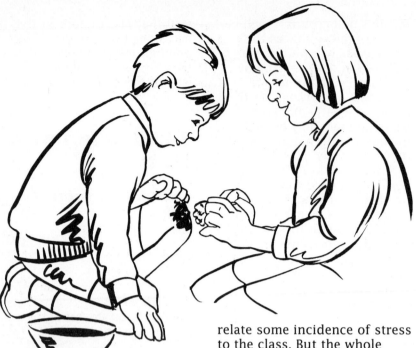

eviction, family violence or breakups; in many schools, children who arrive as refugees have often witnessed or suffered extreme violence. Such stress may be the cause of difficult behaviour – it is important for other children to recognise that such behaviour is often a natural reaction to undue stress, and that individuals under stress need to be tolerated and helped rather than ostracised and punished.

You will need to make some sensitive judgements about how much of a child's background it is morally acceptable and wise to raise in class. If, for example, a child has been bereaved of a parent, it would usually seem quite proper to tell the other children this before the child returned to school, to discuss with them how it must feel to loose a parent in this way, and what they might do to help.

On the other hand, it would be insensitive to ask a child to relate some incidence of stress to the class. But the whole class could be invited to discuss some related topic (for example, refugees in wartime) and if, for example, the Bosnian or Kurdish child in the class chose to talk about what had happened to them, this would normally be acceptable.

Talking about the way in which stress can affect individuals may help: post-traumatic stress syndrome is now widely recognised, with effects such as tearfulness, bouts of aggression, feelings of paranoia, loss of temper and so on.

# 15. Cuts and scratches

## Foundation subject links
Science.

## Age range
Five to nine.

## Group size
Pairs.

## What you need
Cotton wool, water, a clean bowl, plasters, red ink, an old small make-up sponge.

## What to do
Talk about what happens when someone cuts or grazes themselves:
• why it is painful (to warn you that whatever you did was dangerous);
• why cuts bleed (the breaking of the tubes that take the blood around the body);
• how cuts heal (flushing out any dirt that has got in, clotting and forming a scab of dried blood under which new skin can form).

Talk about how the body can, for most small cuts and scratches, heal itself perfectly well. Cleaning the wound can make things safer and the healing faster.

Make up a 'graze' on a volunteer's knee by dabbing on red ink with a sponge. Demonstrate how to clean it with water using cotton wool to gently stroke away from the wound. Ask for suggestions as to why you use a fresh cotton wool surface for each stroke, and why the strokes are away from the wound.

Allow the children to try out the technique. It takes experience to get enough water on the cotton wool to be effective, but not so much that the victim gets wet socks. Stress the need to call for adult help wherever possible.

## Further activity
Talk about how plasters can keep dirt and bacteria out of wounds, but also slow down the formation of scabs. Talk about bigger cuts and how to stop these bleeding by applying pressure on the wound and elevation until expert help can be summoned.

# 16. Burns and scalds

## Foundation subject links
Science.

## Age range
Five to nine.

## Group size
Pairs.

## What you need
Access to cold running water, soft non-fluffy dressings (if available).

## What to do
Talk about how burns cause pain, swelling and blistering of the skin. The blister of water under the skin allows new skin to form to replace the damaged area while still keeping the body safe from infection. Emphasise the need to keep the blister intact to help the new skin form. If the skin is broken, adult help is needed.

Pain can be relieved by holding the affected area under flowing cold water. When the pain has eased a little (and it may take at least ten minutes under the cold tap), a clean, soft non-fluffy dressing can be used to protect the larger area of blistered skin.

Demonstrate this and ask the children to practise in pairs. Stress the need to summon adult help.

# 17. Younger children

## Foundation subject links

English, science, mathematics.

## Age range

Nine to eleven.

## Group size

Three to five.

## What you need

Access to younger children; rulers and tape measures; reading books for young children; paper, pencils.

## What to do

Talk with the class about how young children develop from the age of about four. Children will suggest changes in size (height and weight), in abilities, and in understanding and knowledge.

Ask them to make a study of these sorts of changes by looking at and talking with younger children. If possible, arrange for each group to work with a child 'borrowed' from one of the younger classes. Ideally, they could look at three or four different-aged children, in turn, over a few days.

They should measure the children's height and weight, record their shoe size and, with the help of a calculator, work out the ratio of the size of the head to the height of the body. By pooling the information collected by the groups, averages can then be calculated.

The younger children could also be asked what they are able to do – tie shoelaces, thread a needle, go home from school on their own and so on. They could also be gently tested on their knowledge – reading, ability to calculate change and so on.

Gradually, the children in your class should build up a picture of how younger children grow and of the kind of things and attention they need in order to develop well.

Each group could make a book on children's development in which they could record their findings.

## Further activities

The children could make a more systematic study, looking at all the children in each class; plot graphs of growth and bar charts of changes in ability; use a computer database to keep track of the results and to analyse them.

# 18. Dem bones, dry bones

### Foundation subject links

Science.

### Age range

Seven to eleven.

### Group size

Pairs.

### What you need

Photocopiable page 173, pencils.

### What to do

Explain that each pair is going to explore how their muscles work to move their bodies. Muscles are attached to bones and move the bones by pulling one against the other.

The first picture on photocopiable page 173 shows the upper arm and its muscles. Ask the children to identify the parts with their partner. When they move their arms up or down, they use different muscles to pull one way or the other. Ask them to find out which muscles pull which way. Get them to try pulling up against something very heavy or fixed. Which muscles are used? Ask them to feel around the upper arm as the pulling starts and to draw in the flexed muscles on the second picture. Then they could try pushing down with the arm and observe which muscles are used. They should draw these in the third picture.

Discuss how muscles can only contract and pull bones towards each other. They cannot push them apart – another muscle must contract to pull them in the opposite direction.

### Further activity

Let the children try out movement in other parts of the body, for example, the leg, the forearm or the hand.

## 19. Fat

### Foundation subject links
Science.

### Age range
Seven to eleven.

### Group size
Pairs.

### What you need
A selection of fats and oils, and foods that contain some of them such as crisps, and peanuts. Ensure that any vegetarians in the class do not work with animal fats; that Muslim and Jewish children do not come into contact with pork products and that Hindu children do not come into contact with beef fat. You will also need filter or blotting paper for testing and soap for cleaning up.

### What to do
Fats are an important part of our diet. Some come from animal products and others from vegetables. Ask the children to make a list of all the edible fats and oils that they know. They could classify these into sets of animal and plant derivatives. Some butter and margarine substitutes ('spreads') are a mixture of both. Children could bring in labels from fat products to examine the constituents and origins of each.

A simple (though not always conclusive) test for the presence of fats is to smear a substance on blotting or filter paper. Fats make the paper translucent. This works well with oils and spreads and will also allow animal fat, for example, suet, to be examined and seen to contain fat.

Children may mention that there are different kinds of fats, saturated and unsaturated. The latter are considered the healthier of the two because they are less likely to lead to the formation of deposits in the circulatory system, which in turn leads to arterio-sclerosis. Children could classify saturated and unsaturated fats, using food labels as an indicator.

### Further activity
Discuss that, while we all need to eat some fats to stay healthy, too much of any type of food is not healthy.

## 20. Food types

### Foundation subject links
Science, English.

### Age range
Seven to eleven.

### Group size
Three to five.

## What you need
A range of foodstuffs and contents labels, pencils.

## What to do
There are a number of ways of classifying foods. For example, foods from animal products and those from vegetable products (there are also a few of mineral origin). One of the most useful ways of classifying foods is dividing them into the various components needed for a healthy diet:
• carbohydrates – can be broken down to provide energy (sugars and starches, in fruit, sugar, bread, potatoes, pasta, rice);
• proteins – used to construct different parts of the body (pulses, eggs, meat);
• fats – used both for energy and for body-building and repair (of vegetable and animal origin);
• vitamins – various kinds found in various foodstuffs, needed in very small quantities to maintain health.

Many of these food substances can be manufactured by our bodies. We can use carbohydrates to make most (but not all) proteins, for example. If we have eaten too much food, the extra can be converted to fat and laid down in layers in our body as a store, in case we go hungry. Fats can be broken down to build energy-releasing sugars or to make many proteins. We cannot make some proteins and we cannot make most of the vitamins (vitamin D is an exception because our bodies can produce it if our skin is exposed to sunlight).

Ask the children to analyse the contents of various meals and foodstuffs in terms of their carbohydrate, protein, fat and vitamin content. Food labels that list nutritional information can be most useful here.

Ask the children to list the food that they have eaten over the past 24 hours and see how much of a dietary balance they have achieved.

## Further activity
Discuss the need for a healthy food intake. The problems of over- and undereating are in some cases established in childhood and an attitude towards sensible eating can be developed at this age if one takes care not to encourage feelings of anxiety over food intake and body size.

## 21. Passive smoking

### Foundation subject links
Science, English.

### Age range
Seven to eleven.

### Group size
Four to six.

### What you need
Materials for making posters.

### What to do
Ask the children about things that they can smell. Can they smell cigarette smoke? Discuss with them the dangers of smoking (see Activity 4 on page 62). If smoke from cigarettes is dangerous to smokers, is it going to be safe for other people who have to breathe in the same air, even though it has been diluted?

Many children will have heard of passive smoking. It is referred to in some of the government health warnings on cigarette advertisements and packets. How can passive smoking be avoided? What can be done to control smoking in areas where people may have to smoke passively?

Ask the children to make posters pointing out the dangers of passive smoking. Talk about controlling smoking in public areas, for example, on trains and buses or in shops.

### Further activity
Collect information about the dangers of smoking.

## 22. Air pollution

### Foundation subject links
Science, English.

### Age range
Five to eleven, with adaptations as necessary.

### Group size
Four to six.

### What you need
Muslin, elastic, white tiles, petroleum jelly, photocopiable page 174.

### What to do
Discuss air pollution with the class. Ask the children to suggest causes for this kind of pollution such as vehicle exhausts, power generation, manufacturing. While we need these activities to go on, we also need to minimise the pollution that they cause. Can air pollution be detected? Can the children see dirty air?

Ask the children to investigate ways of measuring pollution in the air in different places. Muslin masks (secured with elastic to cover the nose and mouth) can be used to show the visible dirt normally breathed in. Alternatively, do-it-yourself stores sell cheap disposable masks that may be used. After using a mask for an hour or so, the children should compare it to the colour of muslin that has not been used. This activity may work best outside in a busy street.

If white tiles are smeared with a thin layer of petroleum jelly, they will pick up particles in the air. The children should set tiles up in different places, for example, near and far from a busy road, and then compare these to an unused tile after 24 hours. Which areas show the least pollution? Could a map be drawn to demonstrate this?

Lichens on trees also respond and grow differently according to the background level of air pollution. Longer and more filament-like lichens grow in cleaner air. The pictures on photocopiable page 174 show some of the varieties and the degree of air pollution that they represent.

### Further activity
The children could look at other forms of air pollution such as acid rain. The Meteorological Office forecasts now often include an air quality report, noting when levels of air pollution are likely to be high.

# 23. Food additives

## Foundation subject links
Science, English.

## Age range
Nine to eleven.

## Group size
Three to five.

## What you need
Food labels, a list of food additive numbers and their names, paper, pencils.

## What to do
Ask groups of children to examine the labels from prepared foods and to list the additives that they contain. Deciding what is an additive and what is not is not straightforward and you will need to discuss this, and encourage children to exercise their judgement.

Additives are used to preserve food (for example, salt, sugar), to provide flavour and to add colour. Some additives have been used for many centuries, while many others are more recent. The list of 'E' ingredients was devised as a way of ensuring that consumers knew what they were eating, and were not fobbed off with 'colouring matter'. This was important, because some additives cause allergies in some people. Foodstuff labels now usually contain a mixture of numbers, product names and words describing their use.

Which foodstuffs contain lots of colouring matter? Which foods have their own colour? Which foods require flavourings or 'enhancers'?

## Further activity
Investigate food preservation in the past.

# 24. Starch test

## Foundation subject links
Science.

## Age range
Seven to eleven.

## Group size
Pairs.

## What you need
Small quantities of bread, potato, carrot, vegetable oil, rice (cooked if possible), egg white, orange juice; iodine in a dropper bottle, white tiles, small test tubes or beakers, small glass rods for mixing.

## What to do
Different foods contain different amounts of starch. Starch can be detected with iodine. A drop of iodine solution will go dark violet if it is put into contact with starch. Ask the children to test out a range of foodstuffs with iodine. Which ones contain starch and which ones do not? Is there a difference in reaction between very starchy and less starchy foods?

Starches are broken down in the body into simpler sugars that do not give this purple reaction. The process begins in the mouth – it is one of the first stages of digestion. Children can examine this taking place. One child in each pair should collect some saliva in a test tube or beaker. He should then put a drop of saliva on a corner of the tile and test it with iodine. Now ask the children to add some bread to the saliva and mix it with the glass rod. They should put a drop of this mixture on another place on the tile and test it. It will show that the bread is full of starch.

After a minute, ask them to test another drop of the mixture with iodine, and then another drop a minute later and so on. Gradually, the mixture will become less and less purple and stay yellow. This shows how the saliva (or agents within it) have digested the starch. This is the first stage of making the food simple enough to be absorbed by the body.

## Further activity
Try the same tests with rice or mashed potato. Is saliva equally effective with these?

# 25. Growing up

## Foundation subject links
English, science.

## Age range
Nine to eleven.

## Group size
Four to eight. Some schools or teachers may prefer or require groups separated into boys and girls.

## What you need
A collection of magazine and newspaper pictures of people of different ages from childhood to old age, but perhaps with a particular emphasis on the 10 to 20 age range. Both sexes and several ethnic backgrounds should be represented.

## What to do
Begin with some simple sorting activities: the children may sort the pictures into male or female, or black and white or colour, for example.

When the children are familiar with the pictures, ask the groups to sort out the pictures in what they think is age order. Ask them how they know some people are older than others.

Ask them to list some of the ways in which older teenagers differ from people of the children's own age. Encourage them to respond with a variety of characteristics: behaviour, tastes, understanding, things that they are legally able to do and so on, as well as physical characteristics. They could then sort their list out into different headings.

Talk with the children in small groups about the physical changes they have noticed that happen to boys and girls as they enter their teens. Reassure them that such changes occur at quite different times for different individuals; there is no 'normal' age. Link this work to the school's formal sex education programme.

**NB** Note the legal requirements for governors to determine a sex education policy, as noted in the background chapter (page 53). Make sure that you are complying with school policy.

## Further activity
Girls in Years 5 and 6 need to understand and be ready for the beginning of menstruation. Boys also need to be aware of this phenomenon.

# 26. Safety in the kitchen

## Foundation subject links
Science, technology, English.

## Age range
Seven to eleven.

## Group size
Four to six.

## What you need
A collection of kitchen items to examine and photographs or pictures of items that cannot be brought into the classroom; paper, pens, felt-tipped pens.

## What to do
Ask the children to examine one of the items (or its picture) – knives, saucepans, tin-openers, cookers and so on. Can they identify all the possible dangers associated with the item's use? They might like to also consider if the item in question poses any special problem for the elderly or the very young.

Ask the group to make up a set of simple rules about using the item that might help avoid dangers. When they have surveyed several items, ask them if they can identify groups of similar objects, which present similar potential dangers. Can they make warning logos that alert kitchen users to particular hazards – hot surfaces, boiling liquids, sticky surfaces, or fragile items, for example?

## Further activity
Ask the children to design a kitchen that minimises hazards.

# 27. Internal transport system

## Foundation subject links
Science, technology, English.

## Age range
Nine to eleven.

## Group size
Initially small groups, then the whole class.

## What you need
Card or sugar paper, empty matchbox trays (or something similar), a shoebox, paper fasteners, Plasticine, scissors, glue.

## What to do
This activity, which will eventually involve all the class, makes a model that shows how blood circulates in the human body. The model should ideally be constructed in several stages, and will temporarily occupy a large floor space in the classroom.

### Stage 1: the system of arteries and veins
Ask the class to cut strips of thick sugar paper or card, 60cm × 15cm. The ends of each strip should be rounded. Ideally, the paper or card should be pale yellow (plasma-coloured). At least 20 strips are needed. Each strip is fitted to the next one with a paper fastener, to form a long articulated strip about 10m long. One group should also make a small bridge from a cardboard shoebox.

This 'bloodstream' should then be arranged in a figure-of-eight system, with the

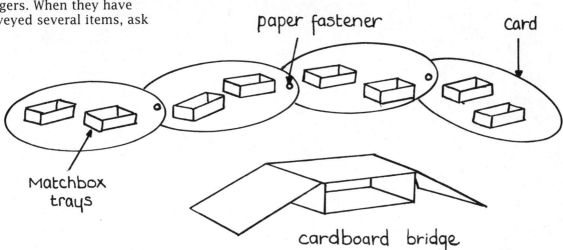

paper fastener

card

Matchbox trays

cardboard bridge

cardboard bridge allowing one stream to pass over another. This cross-over point represents the heart, with one stream of blood leaving to the lungs and then returning to the heart, to be sent out in another stream to the body.

Ask the children to place themselves around the circuit, so that they can move the strip on, thus imitating the flow of blood.

### Stage 2: moving oxygen and carbon dioxide
Stick two small matchbox 'trays' to each part of the strip. These represent red blood cells. A group of children can represent the lungs, and put Plasticine blobs of 'oxygen' into the trays as they go past them. Other children, representing the body section of the track, can remove the oxygen as the blood passes them, to allow the body to work. Oxygen can be replaced

with carbon dioxide Plasticine blobs (using a different colour), which will not go in the trays, being instead carried dissolved in the plasma. When the blood returns to the lung area, the lung group can remove the carbon dioxide (and exhale it), and put more oxygen into the blood cells.

The circulation of gases around the body is now demonstrated.

### Stage 3: other functions of the blood
Other sections along the 'body' length of the circulatory track can now be designated: there could be a stomach, which puts in water and food, with a liver a little farther along which takes out food, stores it and produces a regular stream of sugars for the rest of the body to use. Kidneys take out

excess water (always leaving some in circulation) and waste products. The rest of the body – several groups of children along the track – could extract sugars as well as oxygen, replacing them with waste materials and water, as well as carbon dioxide. Each substance will need to be represented with a different colour of Plasticine, and introduced and discussed separately, so that a complex pattern is eventually built up, showing the many functions of the bloodstream.

### Further activity
The children could mount the system on the wall and add labels.

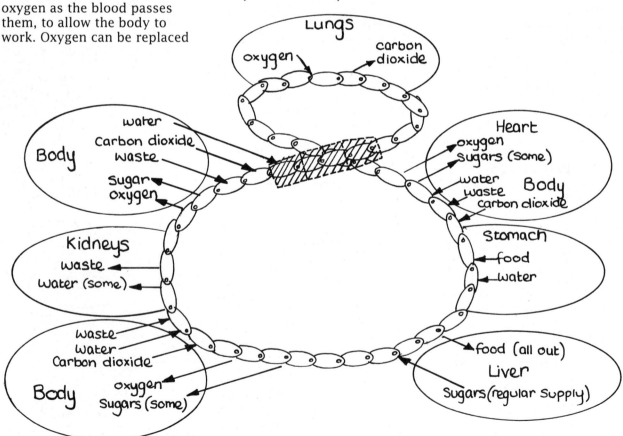

# CHAPTER 3

# Careers education and guidance

Of all the cross-curricular themes, careers education and guidance has seemed to several commentators to be the least appropriate for primary schools. There are perhaps three reasons for these objections. First, many of those working in the primary school culture resist the idea that they are 'preparing children for work' and that the curriculum offered in schools should be some form of training for work. Second, many adults recall the careers guidance that they received, almost invariably in the later years in secondary education, and cannot see how this could sensibly translate into work with younger children. Finally, this particular cross-curricular theme does overlap with that of education for economic and industrial awareness, at least as far as the primary child is concerned.

Nevertheless, there are some cogent reasons why primary children (including infants) need to have some experience of considering their future and possible roles in society. Her Majesty's Inspectorate put it thus: 'Careers Education and Guidance is needed by all pupils [...] and the groundwork for it needs to be carried out from the primary years onwards.' (Curriculum Matters 10: Careers Education and Guidance, 1988 DES). The arguments for careers education (if not for guidance) in primary education will be explored in this chapter.

# BACKGROUND

In the introduction, three possible objections to careers education for primary children were identified:
• primary children should not be 'prepared' for employment;
• careers education is about selecting specific jobs;
• this area is no different from economic and industrial understanding.

Primary children certainly do not need to be prepared for employment. But even at a preschool age, they are beginning to be aware of different types of employment and of whom is carrying them out. Stereotypical views of work are formed during the primary years. Children often see people of particular age, ethnic group, class and/or gender in particular types of employment or unemployment, and project their vision of themselves into similar roles. This drastically limits the opportunities, motivations, ambitions and ultimate success of many children. So while children do not need to be trained for employment, they do need to be encouraged to see themselves positively. They

need to see how they could project themselves into a number of different career roles and to see that it is possible for individuals to change and to choose.

Careers education certainly used to be very much directed at selecting a specific career or job. But the changing nature of employment has affected the nature of careers education. There are far fewer jobs available than there were 20 years ago. Employees and employers expect that people will change jobs and careers several times in a working lifetime. Some of the more recent changes of emphasis in this field have therefore focused on developing skills of adjustment to change: self-reliance, adaptability, flexibility and problem-solving. More people are likely to have several different careers, as well as more than one employer for each career, and to have periods of unemployment and retraining between careers. It is therefore

more important for people to have a sense of their own identity outside their work role. These notions – of transition and change, of self and identity, and of work and careers – are the central foci of the new careers education.

In the case of primary children, there certainly is an area of overlap between some of these issues and those raised in economic and industrial awareness (see Chapter 2). But there are a number of subtle differences of emphasis which will be developed over the rest of this chapter.

Although careers education in the primary school does not have the same overwhelming urgency and priority as the other cross-curricular themes, it is still an important area in which young children can be

first empowered to exercise choice, develop a sense of self-awareness and project themselves into positive roles.

## Careers education: aims and objectives

Careers education has four objectives over the period of full-time education:
• to allow pupils to know themselves better, to be aware of their potential, their likes and dislikes, and their options;
• to make pupils aware of the range of educational and training opportunities, and their relevance to career opportunities;
• to give pupils skills of making choices and decisions about their own continuing education and training, within and beyond compulsory schooling, and the relationship of these choices to career paths;
• to give pupils the skills and attitudes necessary to manage transitions to new roles and situations.

Although all of these have some relevance to the primary school, the first and the fourth objective are most directly applicable in the years up to the age of eleven. Within these four objectives, the National Curriculum Council document *Curriculum Guidance Six: Careers Education and Guidance* (1990) usefully suggests five principal strands to be developed.
• Self: knowledge of self-qualities, attitudes, values, abilities, strengths, limitations, potential and needs.
• Roles: positions and expectations in relation to family, community and employment.
• Work: application of productive effort, including past employment and unpaid work in the community and at home.
• Career: sequence of work roles undertaken through working life and the personal success, rewards and enjoyment it brings.
• Transition: development of qualities and skills which

enable people to adjust to and cope with change, for example, self-reliance, adaptability, flexibility, decision-making, problem-solving.

Within the primary curriculum, these strands need be developed so that children are aware of their own potential and possibilities. It is in these years that important attitudes and generalisations about work and careers are formed, and there is evidence to show that many children arrive at decisions that certain occupations and careers are not suitable or possible for people of their particular background or capabilities. These decisions often are reflections of wider social stereotypes and simply limit children's opportunities and potential in the future. These views will be arrived at from general social observation of their local environment, and particularly from stereotypes of work reflected in television programmes. For example, many children, during the primary years of schooling, arrive at fairly firm opinions about what sorts of jobs are 'men's work' and what sorts are 'women's work', and which

jobs could be done by either men or women. Girls are more likely to see a wider range of occupations open to them than boys. The majority of boys aged nine to eleven have quite strong conceptions of certain work as being only available to men. Girls also may limit themselves, often going against direct family experience. For example, one nine-year-old girl whose mother was a doctor and who knew a great deal about her work, insisted that only men could be doctors. Children from particular ethnic or cultural groups may also see their work possibilities limited in stereotyped ways because of racial prejudice. Some children may perceive that people from their background do not stay in education beyond the school-leaving age or acquire qualifications, and this may lower their own expectations and limit their career development and potential (see *Learning to Labour*, P. Willis [1978] Saxon).

Primary schools can do much to counter the development of stereotypes. It could be argued by some that it is unwise and unnecessary to raise children's aspirations and hopes, particularly at a time when we do not have full employment and many people will not find work. Unrealistic aspirations, it is argued, will lead to frustration as raised ambitions are thwarted. However, the tackling of stereotypes will mean that more children do not unnecessarily limit themselves and if this happens within a general programme of self-awareness and self-assessment, the individual will be able to realise fully his or her capabilities.

## Careers education from five to seven

In the infant years, children should be extending their awareness of work in the home and in their immediate environment, particularly in school. They will gather together and form generalisations from a small number of experiences. Similarities and differences between different kinds of work will be noticed and categorised. Features of jobs will be distinguished – working out-of-doors, working at home or working in uniform. Often such generalisations will be held with remarkable tenacity. Jobs will be seen in very distinct terms: good and bad, popular and unpopular. As the children talk with adults about their work, such clear-cut distinctions may become blurred. This can be the time to use job descriptions that are not gender specific – firefighter, police officer or lollipop-person, for example, rather than fireman, policeman or lollipop-lady.

Much of this generalisation is expressed through imaginative role-play based on information and impressions of adult life. Stories that contain descriptions of adults at work may begin to develop wider attitudes. The National Curriculum Council suggest that in the infant years children need to:
• begin to form impressions about themselves;
• develop and describe ideas about roles at work;
• develop and describe ideas about work;
• begin to appreciate the nature of change (transition).

Each of these aims can be translated into activities in a variety of ways in the infant classroom.

Children will begin to develop an impression of their identity and become self-aware as they recognise that they are learning from their own experiences. This is compounded when their developing achievements are recorded and recognised by others, and when they learn to enjoy their work, and discuss and value their different experiences in conversation with others.

Ideas about the different roles that adults have will develop as tasks and jobs around the school are discussed and investigated. Job titles should be explored and a vocabulary to describe aspects of work will develop. Much of this can take place in the context of group activities (contributing also to a sense of self-identity and role within a set of peers). Understanding of what work involves should develop as the children talk with adults. They should then begin to collect a variety of viewpoints about work; also, some challenging of adult stereotypes may begin.

Changes in the local area can be explored through talking with older adults about how their working lives have changed. This emphasis on the recent past will help children to develop the idea that working lives may change in the future, not simply that work was different then from what it is now. This can be extended beyond the school by visiting a local workplace and talking to workers there about their different roles, what they like and dislike about their work and how people work together as a team to achieve a common goal.

## Careers education from eight to eleven

Junior children should be widening and extending their knowledge and awareness of adult working life. Increasingly, they will be describing work in more complex ways, using, for example, different axes by which they classify work:
• paid/unpaid,
• interesting/boring,
• manual/non-manual,
• working for others/working for self.

Jobs will also be classified in other terms, for example: outdoor work, working with particular kinds of equipment, working with animals, jobs that suit particular talents. Children will also see jobs in terms of projections of themselves and consider what they might do in the future: sometimes in the form of fantasy, and sometimes as a self-appraisal of their own potential and possibilities. These will involve considering what they like and do not like doing. As they talk with more adults and as they discuss matters with each other, children will develop clearer ideas about why people work or seek to work. They will also be aware of the level of unemployment, of what this means to people who wish to work and of some of the reasons for unemployment. They will also know about work beyond their own immediate locality and see how they and others are dependent upon these more distant roles.

The National Curriculum Council suggest that at this stage the following four areas should form the focus:
• increasing self-awareness and forming ideas about personal preferences;
• extending understanding about the variety of work roles and their interrelationships;
• exploring various kinds of work, identifying feelings people associate with work, carrying out simple classifications of categories of work;
• preparing pupils for changes

brought about by moving to a new school.

A variety of activities will help achieve these aims in the junior years. Children's experiences of their own development and understanding should be a starting point for developing self-awareness and esteem. The children should be encouraged to review their own work and progress over the years (or even from earlier in the same year) to develop a real sense of progress and success. They should be encouraged to consider their attitudes to work (the parts that were enjoyed or gave satisfaction, the parts that did not), to develop a critical awareness of their achievements and current limitations. This may help in setting the children's personal goals and targets. Children's vocabulary for describing themselves should increase in terms of attitudes and self-awareness. Discussions with their peers about their strengths and about areas still in need of development can be useful in this respect (particularly if in the context

of groups of children engaged in problem-solving tasks). The kind of group work in which members are asked occasionally to stand back and reflect on the processes of working together (and not merely the problem they are working on) helps children clarify the need for working co-operatively, allows individuals to sometimes take the initiative and sometimes work with others, and provides valuable feedback of other people's perceptions.

Junior children should be aware of discrimination and its effect on restricting access to certain employment opportunities. They should discuss issues such as gender and racial stereotyping in employment and, where appropriate, with adults in employment. It is better to allow and help children to raise issues such as these than to pretend that discrimination does not exist: such an attitude will simply alienate many children. Surveys could be conducted of stereotypes in advertising, which might alienate or affect the employment prospects of groups of people – those of a particular gender, racial background or those with special needs.

Children will be increasingly aware of how they and other people work together in teams,

in which different members have different roles. This might be based around some experience of visiting a workplace, where children can talk with various people about the contributions that they make and the contributions that they expect their colleagues to make. It will also arise, as suggested above, through children's own assessment of themselves as members of a team.

Different work opportunities in the local area may be identified by junior children. They should be increasingly aware of the varieties of work and employment and to be able to classify these according to type. Through such activities their conception of work will widen and they may be able to match their own current personal preferences to particular types of work. They should become aware of the range of views on different kinds of work and understand the social and economic values people put on their own work. Such studies should extend to consider work in different cultures and at different times, so that they see how opportunities for work have changed and how different locations offer different job opportunities. Junior children's vocabulary for describing aspects of work should increase, particularly in their analyses of different people's satisfaction or dissatisfaction with their work.

Towards the upper end of the junior school, children will be seeing themselves in a position of transition as they prepare to move to secondary school. This identification of change in their lives may be associated with past events and those transitions yet to come.

# ACTIVITIES

## 1. What I like

### Foundation subject links
English, mathematics.

### Age range
Five to seven.

### Group size
Individuals, pairs and groups of four.

### What you need
Photocopiable pages 175 and 176 cut into twelve individual pictures, mounted on card if you wish; a large sheet of paper or building bricks; scissors, adhesive.

### What to do
This activity is designed to help children discuss their personal likes and dislikes and to achieve a sense of their own value and identity.

Ask each child to look at the pictures and to decide what the children in each of them are doing. Ask them to imagine that they are the child in the picture. Do they think that they would like to do the same thing, would they not like to do it or are they not sure?

They should then arrange the cards into three piles: 'Like', 'Not sure' or 'Don't like'. Or they could put all twelve pictures into order, with the activity that they most like doing at one end, and the one that they least like at the other.

Ask pairs of children to compare their piles or lists and to see if there are differences. Ask groups of four to compare how the pairs are different. Does anyone in the class have exactly the same order?

Discuss with the children why people like doing different things. Then discuss whether there are things that people dislike but have to do. Read and discuss stories in which the characters have strong likes and dislikes.

### Further activity
Make graphs of the most popular and the least popular activities in the class. Do this either with children's individual pictures on squares of paper stuck to a large sheet; or by using building bricks (one brick per child) stacked up in different piles for different activities (use the printed pictures to identify the activity).

## 2. Workers around us

### Foundation subject links
English, geography.

### Age range
Five to nine.

### Group size
The whole class, often working in groups of about six.

### What you need

A camera and film, paper and pencils, felt-tipped pens, clipboards, an enlarged map of the local area (very large scale with just two to three roads for the younger children), materials for a wall chart and class book.

### What to do

Take the class to look for people working in the locality around the school. You might like to discuss what they mean by 'at work'. They could include shoppers and childcarers, as well as people in paid employment (including people driving commercial and other vehicles).

Ask the children to draw and/or photograph each person that is seen and to try to identify their job. If possible, the children could talk with them about their work, how often they are in the locality, who they work for and so on.

In class, ask the children to make a wall chart showing where the different workers were seen, using a map of the locality. Discuss each job in turn:

• who worked on their own, who worked in a team;
• who was a regular worker in the area, who was only an occasional visitor;
• who was an outdoor worker, who usually worked indoors;
• who was paid and who was not.

### Further activities

Make a class book of local workers, with pictures, names and brief job descriptions.

Try the same activity in a different season of the year. Are there different workers about? How does the climate affect their jobs?

## 3. Jobs in the community

### Foundation subject links

English, geography.

### Age range

Seven to eleven.

### Group size

The whole class, then groups of about six.

### What you need

A large sheet of paper (optional); materials for a class book.

### What to do

Ask the class to consider all the services that are provided in the school and the area around it. These might include the provision of services and power (water, electricity, gas, sewerage, telephones, refuse collection); teaching, cleaning, catering and building maintenance within the school; road repairs; street-crossing assistants; policing; social services; and so on. Encourage the children to think as widely as possible.

List all these services on one side of the chalkboard or on a large sheet of paper. Then ask the class to consider who provides each of these services. Can they list the workers concerned? In some cases, they may be able to suggest names of people they have seen; at other times, they will infer that there must be people providing the service whom they have not seen. Some services may have more than one worker.

Finally, ask the groups to consider how each person on the list is employed and paid. How are these services provided and how does the community get what it needs? Who decides?

### Further activity

Invite some of the people whom the children have mentioned into school to talk about their work with the children. The class or groups could make books about the people they have spoken to, describing the various activities that they do in a day.

# 4. Changes, changes

## Foundation subject links
English, history, technology.

## Age range
Seven to eleven.

## Group size
Ideally, not more than eight in a group – but it may be necessary to have half the class working with a visitor at the same time.

## What you need
Access to people who have worked for about 30 or more years and who are willing and able to talk about their working life with the children; a cassette recorder, a camera, paper, pencils, felt-tipped pens, paint, paintbrushes.

## What to do
The nature of most individual jobs has changed quite dramatically over the past 30 years and even more so since the 1930s. This activity involves children gathering information about the types of changes that have taken place.

Ideally, several people who could offer different experiences of change should be invited into school to talk to the children about the following issues:
• Social change: women's roles in workplaces continue to change as employment and promotion opportunities open up. What has this meant for women at work? Are they still responsible for the domestic work and child-raising, as well as paid employment?
• Technological change: new machinery and equipment have altered the nature and patterns of work; office workers can now be based at home, using electronic equipment; new kinds of work have been created; many manual jobs have become physically easier but require new and different skills.
• Economic change: as the economy has changed, so have the number of workers and types of work – far fewer people work in certain industries (mining, agriculture), while other industries have moved from craft workers to larger-scale, factory-based enterprises.

Ask the children to find out from the visitors what work was like when they started and how it is different now. What were the causes of the changes? Do they like them?

The children could photograph or draw one of the visitors, or paint pictures of how their work might have been then and how it is now. They could also make a book or a time-line frieze showing the changes and when they occurred.

Ask the children to imagine what changes may happen to them in their adult working lives.

## Further activity
Take the children on a visit to a workplace. Encourage them to talk to the employees about the changes that have happened and how they feel about them.

# 5. When I grow up I will be a...

### Foundation subject links
English.

### Age range
Five to eleven.

### Group size
Individuals, pairs and small groups.

### What you need
Pictures of people working (from magazines, etc.), paper, adhesive, scissors, pens.

### What to do
Ask the children to collect pictures of people working and assemble a class collage showing a wide range of occupations. Use this as an opportunity to talk about the wide range of work that is possible.

Ask the children to think of what sort of job they would like to do. This need not be based on the collage pictures, but their individual choices will invariably have been widened by that activity.

They could draw themselves working in that job, write about the work or make booklets describing how they would get to that position, what they would do and how the job might develop and change as they grew older. Different age groups will need different tasks.

Ask pairs or small groups of children to show each other what they have done and to talk about their ideas and plans.

### Further activity
Ask the class to collect the information about which occupations have been selected. A bar chart could be made to show if there are any particularly popular jobs. Is there any gender-stereotyping evident? Let the class talk about this. (See Activity 7 on page 91.)

# 6. Target-setting

### Foundation subject links
English.

### Age range
Seven to eleven.

### Group size
Individual children paired up with their best friends.

### What you need
Photocopiable page 177 (optional), pencils, paper.

### What to do
This activity helps develop self-esteem as children evaluate their own needs, set targets that are achievable, meet them and then analyse their progress.

Ask the children to work with a friend. In these pairs, they are to think about their best qualities and areas of work. You could suggest different kinds of competencies to them or use photocopiable page 177 as a basis.

How do they and their friends rate their current performances? If the friend

and the child disagree, they must talk it out until they come to a conclusion.

Ask each child to select a few areas in which they do not do so well. You may want to suggest how many – for some children just one target area may be sufficient and feasible. The pair should then set some achievable target for change in a short timespan, perhaps two weeks, perhaps less with younger children. Finally, each child should write down his or her personal goals. These targets are their own and can remain private if they wish.

After the set time period has elapsed, the same pairs should review what progress has been made towards achieving the goals.

The process can then be repeated, setting fresh targets or revising existing ones, in the same areas or in new ones.

# 7. Women's work, men's work?

## Foundation subject links
English, history, technology.

## Age range
Five to eleven, with variations as appropriate.

## Group size
Four to eight.

## What you need
A list of jobs (photocopiable page 178 may be helpful for older children), paper, pencils, rulers.

## What to do
Stereotypes about gender and work emerge very early in life. In this activity, children will consider if they hold any such stereotypes and will try to explain why they hold them.

Present the children with a wide range of occupations. You could use a picture showing lots of people working with younger children or a list such as that on photocopiable page 178 with older ones. Ensure that all children know what each job entails. Be sure to use non-gender-specific language: avoid using 'he' or 'she' and refer instead to 'refuse collectors', 'people who deliver the post' and so on.

Explain that some people think that some jobs can only be done by a man or a woman and that some can be done by either. Ask the groups to

discuss each job and to see if they can agree on which jobs belong in one of three sets:
• men's work;
• women's work;
• men's or women's work.

If the group cannot agree, they have to leave that occupation out of their sorting.

Ask the groups to compare their lists. Are there any jobs which everyone agrees are either only for men or only for women? Do all the groups agree? Why are some jobs seen as being more 'male' or more 'female'? Do the groups of jobs have anything in common?

## Further activity
It would be interesting to arrange for separate groups of boys and girls to undertake the initial sorting and then to open a discussion. This is more likely to show a difference of opinion and to lead to a good discussion.

# 8. Moving on

### Foundation subject links
English.

### Age range
Ten to eleven.

### Group size
About four.

### What you need
Paper, pencils, access to secondary school pupils.

### What to do
In small groups, the children should consider what changes they think will await them when they transfer schools. Will they study different things? Will they study in different ways? Will they make friends? Do they have any concerns about moving on? How will they cope with these changes?

Once they have made their concerns known, these can then be discussed and the children can be prepared for the changes. If possible, arrange for ex-pupils of your school to visit and talk with the class about the realities of the changes that they experienced. You may also want to add your own comments and to involve staff from some of the secondary schools to which your school sends pupils.

Start discussions within the context of changes that happen in life. Ask groups to consider how they remember feeling when they began school and to look forward to how they imagine they will feel on leaving secondary school and so on.

### Further activity
Ask the children to plan out their own autobiographies. Ask them to review the changes they have been through so far and also to project into their possible future in the years ahead.

# 9. A day in the life of...

### Foundation subject links
English, history, geography, technology.

### Age range
Five to eleven, with suitable modifications for younger children.

### Group size
Ideally, no more than eight; larger groups may be necessary in practice.

### What you need
A number of willing adults who will talk to the children about their daily routines; cameras, clipboards, paper, pencils, tape recorders may all be useful; materials for making a book, time-line, frieze or pie-chart.

### What to do
Give each group the task of discovering and recording what a person does in their work throughout the day. The children will need to construct an hour-by-hour record of the day, from waking to bedtime (particularly in considering the working days of parents with young children).

Some primary schools have found it possible for pairs or groups of three children to 'shadow' an appropriate person for part of the working day. They might photograph and/or record aspects of his or her daily work.

Ask the children to find out how much the routine may change from day to day. If the person has been doing the same work for a number of years, how has the daily routine changed?

### Further activity
Ask the children to construct a book, a time-line or a frieze of a day to show the day's events.

Add clock faces or suns and moons to show the passage of time.

Make a pie-chart to show the changes over 24 hours.

# 10. Studying a career

## Foundation subject links
English, technology.

## Age range
Nine to eleven.

## Group size
Individuals.

## What you need
Careers materials, books on different occupations (for example, Hamish Hamilton's *Cherrystones* series), paper, pens, envelopes, stamps.

## What to do
Ask each child to consider what sort of job they would like to do later in life. Ask them to make a serious choice, taking into account their abilities and interests, not just their fancies!

Then ask them each to find out how people achieve that occupation. What qualities does a person need to do the job? Are there skills that have to be learned? How? Are there qualifications? Are there courses to follow – job training or college courses? What has to be done to enrol on such courses?

To find the answers to these questions, each child will need to use reference books, write and/or talk to people doing similar work or write to employment bodies or colleges.

Finding out this information sets out before children the nature and purposes of personal development and progression, and helps to establish the concept of personal goals and stages of development.

## Further activity
Each child could make a forecast of what they would need to do to join their chosen occupation. When would various stages need to be completed? What qualifications and subjects are the most important? They may wish to revise their choice of occupation as a result.

# 11. A worker's biography

## Foundation subject links
History, English.

## Age range
Five to nine.

## Group size
Four to five, but larger groups are possible if access to adults is limited.

## What you need
Access to a number of adults who have had a relatively long working life – say, twenty years or more – ideally with some variety (e.g., domestic/child-rearing, alternating with various full- and part-time employment).

## What to do
The task of the group is to construct a working-life history of the adult they are to interview: what he or she has done, in what order, and for how long. This will help the children understand the ways in which patterns of working life change, and that many people switch roles at different stages in their adult life.

Ask the group to find out all that they can about how the adult enjoyed the particular tasks, why and when they changed, and any advantages or disadvantages that followed from the transitions.

Encourage the children to consider carefully how they will present their information, so that other groups can compare their findings. Would a time-line of some sort be appropriate? Could some colour coding be used to show different kinds of work (paid/unpaid, full-time/part-time)?

Encourage a class discussion of the similarities and differences between the various biographies that have been collected.

### Further activity
Make a large wall chart to compare a number of different people's working-life histories.

# 12. Attributes

### Foundation subject links
English.

### Age range
Seven to eleven (possible for younger children with some adaptation).

### Group size
Pairs or small groups, probably best arranged on a friendship basis.

### What you need
Photocopiable page 179, pencils.

### What to do
This activity encourages children to reflect on their own qualities, skills and attributes, formulating what they consider themselves to be good at.

Working in pairs or small groups, each child has to construct a list of his or her particular abilities. The list on photocopiable page 179 may be useful: the children could either write in comments or draw a picture of themselves doing the activity. The emphasis should be positive, listing and describing things that the child does well or enjoys. Other members of the group can be used to comment on and make suggestions about the list.

Try to discourage some children from 'being good at everything' (this may not help other children see themselves positively): you may need to ask children to limit themselves to identifying only three or four characteristics.

A class or large-group discussion on abilities and differences may be a useful conclusion.

### Further activity
For some activities which involve group work, it may be useful for children to form groups in which there is a range of talents. The attribute sheets can be useful in doing this: children can negotiate membership of groups to ensure that appropriate skills are represented.

# CHAPTER 4

# *Environmental education*

The environment has been important since life on Earth began, but it has never been static. There have been many dramatic life-threatening changes in the past. What makes environmental concerns so important today is the realisation that the changes taking place today are caused by human activity, and are on an unprecedented scale. Not only have the processes that cause most concern accelerated dramatically over the past half-dozen decades, but they are taking place on a global scale, rather than being confined to relatively small pockets in the developed world. While we make these changes happen, it remains to be seen whether we can control them. We appear to have realised, at a very late date, how finely balanced is the equilibrium in which our ecosystem is held.

So what has all this got to do with education? Surely, saving the environment is a matter for scientists and technologists to devise solutions, and for governments and international organisations to regulate and control? This is true up to a point: clearly, most individuals cannot take action to stop such ecological disasters as the oil spillage of the Braer, for example, or Chernobyl. But individuals do have important roles to play.

• It is individuals who make, or fail to make, decisions that lead to ecological disasters and environmental damage. If all individuals were educated to be aware of the environmental impact of their actions, then some decisions would be better informed.

• Individuals can group together to take action that compels company, national and international action. Thus groups such as Greenpeace, Friends of the Earth or the World Wildlife Fund for Nature put pressure, in different ways, on those who can make decisions.

• Individuals take many daily decisions that have a significant (if small-scale) environmental impact. While any one person taking steps to conserve resources, for example, by recycling waste products, has very little effect on global problems, many individuals doing the same thing do begin to have an effect.

This is not to absolve companies and national or international bodies of any responsibility to initiate action. It is essential that they regulate through legislation and tax systems, modify the market system where appropriate and make it possible for even the poorest to behave in an environmentally-sound manner (it is the poorest who cannot afford to be environmentally conscious). But individuals have a role to play, as consumers of resources and as producers of waste. This is where environmental education is important.

# BACKGROUND

There is no clear consensus on many environmental issues, nor any agreement on which are the most important or pressing problems. Some issues seem so slight to the lay person that they appear to be of little consequence, while others seem so great that no action that an individual can take would seem able to affect it.

Faced with both enormities of scale and subtleties of balance, it is hard to see how individuals can be made to feel empowered. Environmental education could easily lead to feelings of despair or alienation. Given the apocalyptic warnings on global warming, ultraviolet radiation, species destruction, acid rain, soil exhaustion and erosion, the accumulation of nuclear and other waste and the depletion of non-renewable resources, it would not be surprising if many young people opted to take no part in the proceedings. Instead, many young people are actively engaged in environmental campaigning, and speak and act to reverse environmental degradation. Many primary children seem to be passionately involved in such issues.

## Objectives of knowledge, skills and attitudes

While environmental issues are often contentious and there are a variety of viewpoints about the causes and effects of changes, some of which may be special pleading from vested interests, there is also a body of knowledge – and perhaps more importantly, procedures for acquiring such knowledge about the environment – which forms a useful basis for making judgements. The National Curriculum Council has set out the following areas of knowledge and understanding which should be covered as a basis for making informed judgements about the environment.

• The natural processes which take place in the environment (the water cycle, atmospheric and seasonal changes, the life cycle of organisms, the energy cycle, photosynthesis, respiration, and decay).

• The impact of human activities on the environment (farming, mining, building, industry): while what humans do remains within the self-balancing natural processes described above, little long-term change will follow. But it is one of the fundamental human characteristics that we have the ability to adapt our environment to make life more comfortable, through the processes that we sometimes call technology. For example, we plant crops, tend animals, make clothing and shelter, and use minerals. All of these have an actual environmental impact. When they become large-scale, they may cause damage. Many of the changes

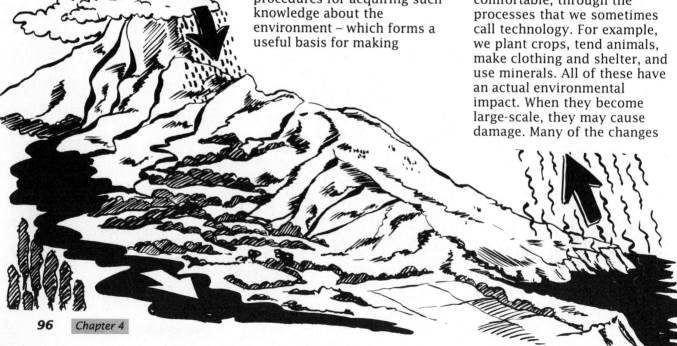

that we make are vital to life: few would argue with creating flood barriers to protect people and their livelihood from destruction, for example, although such action may dramatically affect the local ecological balance. Important and critical moral judgements have to be made about the propriety and value of all our technological activities, and children should begin to be prepared to make such judgements.

• Different environments, both past and present (rivers move, seas flood, climate changes, volcanoes erupt and many human activities are attempts to minimise environmental change): children will need to recognise that many environmental factors are beyond human control and that many changes are inevitable.

• Environmental issues (the greenhouse effect, acid rain, air pollution): there are currently a number of major environmental issues in the area of public concern and debate, but we should expect this list to develop and change over primary children's lifetime. The greenhouse effect, global warming, threats to biodiversity, acid rain, air pollution, the thinning of the ozone layer: some of these may well be resolved within the next decades, but new environmental problems will emerge to take their place. Meanwhile, children need to know, over the course of their schooling, principal issues involved at the moment.

• Local, national and international legislative controls to protect and manage environment; how policies and decisions are made about the environment: most attempts to control the potentially damaging impact that human activity can have on the environment are through national and international controls. Concerted action at a high level of authority is needed to curb the ambitions and activities of individuals and groups who may see their own self-interest as greater than that of society at large.

Children need to see that decisions are being made about environmental control and understand how they are made, as well as the policies and procedures involved.

• The environmental interdependence of individuals, groups, communities and nations: all individuals, groups and nations are environmentally interdependent. The actions of each of us can affect the quality of life of people a long way away, not merely our immediate neighbours. The Scandinavian nations claim that one of the principal causes of acid rain damage in their forests is the emission of sulphurous gases from British power stations, causing acid rain that falls thousands of miles away from its source. Litter thrown by one individual, repeated by dozens of individuals, can threaten the quality of life of many others.

• How human lives and livelihoods are dependent on the environment: changes in climate, for example, could radically alter the ways in which we are able to live. Some environmental changes are through wholly natural causes and others are largely caused by human actions. Increased ultraviolet radiation due to ozone depletion could

eventually lead to massive changes in people's lifestyles.
• The conflicts which can arise about environmental issues: there will very often be conflicts of values and opinions about environmental issues. Very few people consciously want to damage the environment – most of those accused of damage would dispute the facts or claim that they had no alternative. Many people would defend their activities by saying that the degree of what they were doing was insignificant or that in order to survive economically, they had no alternative.
• How the environment has been affected by past decisions and actions: changes in the past affect the environment today. We are always tied to a legacy left by our ancestors. Equally, the decisions we make today will be affecting people hundreds of years in the future.
• The importance of planning, design and aesthetic considerations: effective

planning, with a sensitive awareness of design and aesthetic considerations, can help minimise the possibilities and effects of environmental damage. While we as a species are causing damage on a scale never seen before in history, we are also moving towards controlling environmental damage on a scale not possible before.
• The importance of effective action to protect and manage the environment.

This base of knowledge and understanding about the environment can be used as the basis for the development of the following skills:
• communication – in relaying information and concerns to others;
• numeracy – in collecting data about environmental change and damage and in presenting it;
• study skills – in retrieving information, evaluating it, and in planning environmentally-based projects;
• problem-solving skills – in identifying causes and options and in making balanced judgements;
• personal and social skills – in working co-operatively on

environmental issues and taking responsibility for these;
• information technology skills – in using databases and simulations to record information gathered about an environment or to examine potential outcomes.

All these skills and concepts need to be associated with the development of attitudes such as concern for the care of the environment, independence of thought, concern for the views and feelings of others, respect for evidence, and tolerance and open-mindedness.

## Three approaches

One very useful way of conceptualising the place of the environment within education is to use the following three approaches:
• education *about* the environment (knowledge);
• education *for* the environment (values, attitudes, positive action);
• education *in* the environment (a resource).

The three are inter-connected and develop together but there are different qualities, emphases and reasons for each approach.

### Education about the environment
This refers to an essential knowledge base about our environment. The elements of

green glass
bottle bank

clear glass
bottle bank

brown
bottle bank

the environment (air, weather and climate; land, soil, rocks and minerals; plants, animals, people; water systems, rivers, oceans, clouds, ice) are all linked through both energy systems and through the impact of human activity.

In the English and Welsh National Curriculum, geography includes a very specific identification of environmental geography (AT5): the use and misuse of natural resources; the quality and vulnerability of different environments; and the possibilities for protecting and managing environments. In the science curriculum, there are major references to the process and varieties of life, and to human influences on the earth. It also identifies physical processes relating to energy, materials and their properties, and the earth and its atmosphere, all of which

include knowledge important to the development of an overall understanding of the environment. Design and technology, and history also play a part in developing aspects of this knowledge, enabling children to develop important ideas about how humans have always attempted, in different ways, to manage the environment.

### Education for the environment

Children need more than just knowledge. They need the realisation that they can play a role in caring for the environment and that solutions to environmental problems must be found despite conflicts over values and interests. While informed choice must be based on clear and defined knowledge, it is also inspired and directed by a clear sense of priorities and values. The process of environmental education must include children developing the personal resources necessary to develop, define and implement their values.

Education for the environment is specifically empowering to children. It uses the knowledge they have about the environment and their understanding of the conflicts of values to help them make choices at an individual level:
• to act as an individual;
• to combine together to act in groups;
• to act in an environmentally-responsible manner in a variety of present and future roles;
• to make political and economic decisions that concern the environment in an informed way.

Children will initially be aware of the way their own activities affect the local and familiar environment. The realisation that it is their sweet wrappers that litter the streets is a direct, easy and visible example of cause and effect. Many primary children will also become aware of how their own acts can also have a much wider impact on the regional and even global environment. They may also become aware of how people in positions of industrial, political and economic power can have a very much greater impact.

Such concern and such a definition of values is developed through role-play and discussion in English and drama, through examination of the views and beliefs of others in geography and history, through a consideration of needs and opportunities in design and technology and through the development of aesthetic appreciation in art, music and English.

### Education in the environment

It is necessary and educationally logical to ensure that environmental education takes place in or through the environment. While the school itself is an environmental setting, this should be only one of the locations in which a study of the environment takes place. Direct experience of a variety of environments through visits and school trips, provides very important opportunities to widen children's experiences. These visits need not be designed specifically with environmental education in mind – simply looking and commenting on the areas

being travelled through on the way can help develop some environmental concerns.

Primary children can and should be developing fieldwork practices. A day in a different environmental setting (seaside, farm or city centre) provides opportunities for children of any age to make and record observations, to collect data systematically, and through these to test ideas and predictions, and to make proposals and (where appropriate) decisions for change.

But not all the global environment can be considered through direct experience. Secondary sources (photographs, videos and books) will always have an important part in extending children's awareness and horizons to more distant and inaccessible environments.

## The key topics in environmental education

The National Curriculum Council's document *Curriculum Guidance 7: Environmental Education* (1990) suggests that seven key topics cover the necessary knowledge and understanding:

- climate;
- soils, rocks and minerals;
- water;
- materials and resources, including energy;
- plants and animals;
- people and their communities;
- buildings, industrialisation and waste.

The National Curriculum Council does not suggest any particular way of teaching these topics. They could be approached through the identifiable topics (although they are all entangled one with the other). But it would be equally possible to cover most of environmental education topics through the foundation subjects (particularly geography, but also with elements of history, technology and some science). It would also be possible (and probably more within the primary curriculum tradition) to deliver these topics through projects that have a strong environmental content over a number of terms.

### Climate

The consistent and persistent patterns in the weather form our climate. In the British Isles we have a quite diverse pattern of weather, so that not only does the unpredictability and variation become a cliché of our conversation, but it is not easy for young children to

discern our seasons. The stereotypical winter's day is, in fact, relatively uncommon. For example, some young children in the south of England may have had experience of snow on less than a dozen days in their lives. Conversely, our weather records also show snowfalls as late as 2 June and as early as 25 September.

The climate is not static. It may not appear to change much from year to year, but there are long-term trends. For example, there has been some 400 years of gradual warming since the days when frost fairs could be regularly held on the frozen river Thames each winter. Climatic changes affect the vegetation on Earth and it should be remembered that much of our atmosphere exists because of vegetation. All the free oxygen in the air (one fifth of the total) has come from plants photosynthesising carbon dioxide and water to produce oxygen. Any climatic changes that affect plants (less carbon dioxide, less rainfall, more radiation, impurities such as acidity in the rain) might all upset the delicate balance.

Climatic change also affects humans more directly. Air pollution can make particular localities impossible for humans and whole areas of cities uncomfortable and potentially dangerous. Even more threatening, partly because it is less specific than particular patches of smog or pollution, are the global effects of climatic change. Releasing gases such as CFCs, sulphur dioxide and carbon monoxide into the air leads to serious longer-term effects, for example, the greenhouse effect, in which more radiant heat from the sun penetrates the upper atmosphere because the ozone layer is thinner; and the increasing acidity of rain.

Some of these changes can be tackled relatively simply. CFCs are partly released through aerosol cans and partly through incineration of some kinds of polystyrene packaging. Consumer pressure on manufacturers has led over

the past decade to a dramatic decline in CFC use in this way. Individuals, often banding into pressure groups, have had a significant effect. CFCs are also used in refrigeration. This is more problematic: while manufacturers in developed countries have responded to consumer demands, the costs of alternative refrigeration technologies are too high for some developing countries to bear. Such countries are asking for help in establishing new systems.

Children can be and are involved in such issues. They can not only observe and measure some of the effects of climatic change, but also become involved in exerting pressure on manufacturers and governments.

### Soils, rocks and minerals
There are a wealth of issues concerning the lithosphere.
• The resources that we draw from the earth are often very limited. Extracting gravel, stone and other building materials can play havoc with the environment. There may be plenty of these materials available in the country, but children need to be made aware of the costs of transporting heavy, bulky and relatively inexpensive materials from quarry to building site.
• These scarce resources need to be managed and their use controlled. Market economics may not be the easiest way to do this and often government intervention is needed to limit the use of resources in the wider interest.
• The vulnerability of the soil as a component of the environment needs to be

addressed. Soil erosion is a major problem in some parts of the world and a minority of children, for example those of Bengali or Indian origin, may have direct experience of this. Experimentation with soil types, growing seedlings in different types of soil and examining friability, water and humus content all lie within capability of primary children.

### Water
The essential role of water in plant and animal life is clear and most children appreciate from a young age that pets and plants need regular water supplies to survive. The water cycle is a popular topic in junior schools. It is less common to examine how that cycle can be disturbed and upset, and the environmental consequences that this will bring. The water cycle is normally seen as being in a state of balance. But if water is drawn out of river systems and polluted by agricultural or industrial use before it reaches the sea, then the system could become imbalanced.

A clean water supply is one of the essentials necessary for

human health and children should become aware of the relative ease of access we have to such supplies. Role-play work on gathering and transporting clean water in developing countries can help children to appreciate why water is a precious commodity. In parts of Britain, some children will be aware of and concerned about local droughts, particularly during the summer months.

### Energy
While all life needs energy of some sort, it is only the human species that makes extraordinary demands to use energy. We need energy for a wide variety of purposes: from the simple needs of preparing and cooking food and keeping warm to the more elaborate wants for sophisticated transport, manufacturing and building construction. There may be disagreement about the levels of demand for energy, but we certainly need more than that which our bodies alone can produce. The earliest energy sources were renewable or at least potentially renewable (wood and dung for fuel, water and wind). The discovery of more powerful fuels, which could be economically accessed in an organised manner (particularly coal and oil) led to an enormous expansion in energy use and the provision of goods and services that improved the quality of life. It is only as that

expansion has continued that we have become aware of some of the potential hazards of such a reliance on fossil fuels.

Fossil fuels are finite. It is hard to know how limited they are. Many reserves are currently too expensive to use, but it is possible that technological advances in extraction techniques and the increased price people are prepared to pay for fuel will mean that these reserves will be used later. But there is an ultimate limit on these sources and new reserves of oil and coal will not be available for another hundred million years!

Many junior children become interested in the renewable/non-renewable energy debate, and there is a wealth of competing information and views for children to consider. It is important for children to realise that whatever energy source is adopted, there will

be both environmental and economic consequences. For example, 'wind farms' of giant generators change the appearance of the landscape; dams and power stations for hydroelectric power also will change the existing ecological balance. There are costs and benefits to be balanced.

Power from nuclear fission offers both the advantages of an effectively inexhaustible supply and causing limited environmental damage as far as its generation is concerned. But the problems of safety and of the disposal of spent but highly toxic fuel are such that many people feel that the risks and dangers are too great for these methods to be employed. While this is an area which will interest many older primary children, it has to be examined through indirect experiences. Many organisations are willing to provide information to schools, but teachers need to ensure that a range of viewpoints and information are available for discussion, from Friends of the Earth and Greenpeace, as well as from

British Nuclear Fuels and NIREX.

Energy conservation, on the other hand, is an area where children can get some hands-on experience. Investigations that need little equipment include experiments with letting hot water cool with and without lagging, measuring the energy consumption of different domestic appliances and examining how much rooms need to be heated to be comfortable. These experiments help generate ideas of efficiency and saving, and, coupled with an examination of energy sources, allow children to see how they, as individuals, are in some ways able to influence total energy use.

Much energy generation leads, directly and indirectly, to pollution. Fossil-fuel electricity generators can create fumes that lead to acid rain if they are not fitted with scrubbers that filter out acidic gases. There is now considerable manufacturing interest in reducing car emissions: leaded petrol produces atmospheric lead

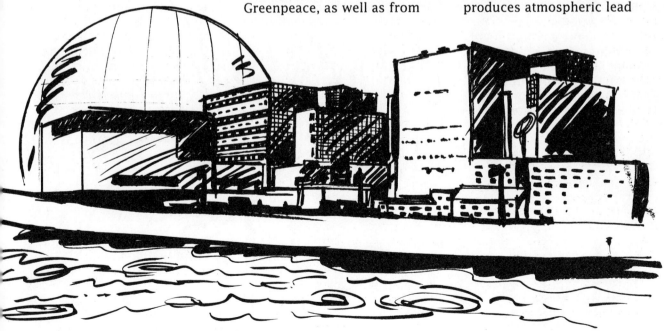

and cars without catalytic converters produce poisonous carbon monoxide, as well as other fumes. All these issues are of interest to children and most older children are aware of them through media and advertising activities.

### Plants and animals

Life on Earth is a delicate balance between species, but at the same time it exists within an environment of change. New life forms emerge and others become less prominent. Sometimes these changes can be relatively sudden, for example, when the dinosaurs became extinct over several million years ago. The changes in the number and balance of species today is happening at a very fast rate, primarily because of the activities of humans.

A concern for the different forms of life is in part motivated by self-interest: upsetting the balance too much could threaten our own existence. But the immediate needs of individual members of our species, and of groups of them, often conflict with the wider self-interest we have in maintaining the equilibrium of living things. It only rarely happens that humans decide deliberately to wipe out an entire species, for example, the destruction of bacterial life-forms such as those responsible for smallpox. The destruction of species at the present rate is largely the result of individual self-interest and ignorance, and the lack of concerted international and national efforts to control these.

The threat to the diversity of life has been popularised through the fate of the Amazonian rainforests, where there is an enormous reserve of unknown plant and animal species. As the forests are destroyed for timber and ranching, many of these species are destroyed, too. The consequences are literally incalculable, but we can point to some of the possibilities: the potential upset of self-balancing life-systems in these environments, the destruction of gene pools from which new species might emerge and the potential loss of useful plants and animals.

Children are particularly concerned when habitats are destroyed: the destruction of the rainforests has been the focus of many school projects. There is also concern for habitats nearer home and this can be linked to the development of wildlife gardens and nature reserves. At the same time, it seems important that children realise that threats to particular habitats are rarely the result of mindless destruction. People who are posing the threats are almost invariably doing so as the result of economic pressures that they find hard to resist.

### People and their communities

Most people are concerned in some way that their environment remains secure for the future. Societies that have a particularly close and symbiotic relationship with the natural environment are perhaps the most acutely conscious of the fragility of that environment and the need to respect it. Sophisticated societies have recently also become aware of threats to the environment through scientific measurements and made this known through modern mass communication. However,

those societies between these two extremes are often least aware of environmental change and its consequences, and least able to take action. The daily struggle for sufficient food and against disease means that short-term measures must be taken in order to survive to the next year, whatever the long-term effects.

The population of the world is increasing at an alarming rate. A very high proportion of the world's population is made up of young people, who will expect, in due course, to have children. People are also living much longer and this means that a much higher proportion of the babies born now will still be alive when they are 60. Even if every couple from now on only has two children, the world's population would be set to increase at least two-and-a-half fold in the next four decades. But the pressure on poor families to have more than two children remains intense. Without systems of state financial social support, people have to rely on their families to provide a social-security network, so the larger the number of children, the more secure that network will appear to be. The environmental consequences of such population growth are potentially catastrophic. The increased demands that will inevitably be made for scarce resources and energy, the increased levels of pollution and industrialisation will challenge us all.

### Buildings, industrialisation and waste

While people have been living in cities for seven thousand years or more, it is only 130 years since there were more urban dwellers than rural dwellers in England. However, by the year 2000, over half the world's population will be living in cities. This poses environmental challenges – for the planning and designing of cities; for the provision of energy, raw materials, water, and for the disposal of waste products.

Industrialisation shifts both the scale and the nature of environmental change: much larger spaces of land are needed; new demands are made on resources; and new forms of effluent are produced, in quantities and concentrations that make it hard for them to be naturally absorbed and recycled.

It is only relatively recently that environmental consequences of city life and industrial life have become a major concern. There have been some individual attempts to manage problems such as by introducing recycling schemes. But national efforts through legislation are set to bring more substantial gains. For example, local authorities now have a target of recycling 50 per cent of the refuse that they collect by the year 2000; and legislation in Germany puts the onus on manufacturers and retailers to deal with the packaging refuse they produce, and for the eventual recycling of their products.

Environmental education presents an important challenge to teachers. It calls for children to be given a sense of empowerment: individually, together and in a variety of roles, now and in the future. It is concerned with children having the ability to make informed judgements and decisions, having the skills to work co-operatively and responsibly, and having attitudes of respect and concern for all aspects of their world.

# ACTIVITIES

## 1. A load of rubbish

### Foundation subject links
Technology, science, mathematics, English.

### Age range
Five to eleven.

### Group size
Whole-class discussions; small groups of four to six for some work.

### What you need
A collection of household rubbish, appropriately made safe (including a good range: some organic material and some paper, metal and glass); disposable plastic gloves; bin liners or boxes; paper; pencils; access and space to store rubbish outside.

### What to do
Explain to the class that they are going to look at the sort of rubbish that an average household wants to get rid of each day.

Display a collection of household rubbish. Ask the children to try and sort out the various kinds of rubbish. They could do this physically (with adequate supervision and wearing gloves) or by making lists with paper and pencil.

Can they think of other things that their household regularly throws out? What about other kinds of rubbish that is disposed of irregularly (old furniture, decorating materials)? What do they think happens to the rubbish? Can they think of other uses for it? What will happen if it is left outside?

If you have space where the rubbish can be safely left outside, arrange for piles of different kinds of rubbish to be left there. Put the piles of rubbish in different boxes or open bin liners and then ask the children to observe what happens to the rubbish over time. Ensure that they do not touch anything or go too close. They could make notes or drawings, or take photographs

of the changes. Which pile of rubbish grows mould and starts to decay? Which rusts? What other changes take place?

Look at the rubbish that the school gets rid of in a week. How much is produced by the children, by the staff room and by the kitchens? You could also analyse the contents of various rubbish bins found around the school.

Discuss whether waste can be cut down, in school and at home. Would sorting it into different types help? Do they use waste paper, bottle bank and aluminium recycling facilities?

### Further activity
Arrange a visit to the local authority's refuse collection depot. It may be possible to visit the contractor's depot, if these services have been privatised. Ask the children to investigate how the rubbish is

sorted and what parts of it are recycled. Where does the rest go? Is it incinerated or used as landfill? Do the depot managers and workers have any ideas or opinions on the eventual destination of all this waste? How much do they get through in a year?

# 2. Changing climates

## Foundation subject links
Geography, history.

## Age range
Nine to eleven.

## Group size
The whole class and small groups.

## What you need
Newspaper reports of extreme weather and climatic change; a world map; reference books on past climates.

## What to do
Discuss the effects of the weather and of different climates on people. You may want to link this to particular local weather events (droughts and hose-pipe bans, storms and flooding). If you teach in the south of England, you might tell the children of your own experiences in the great storms of 1987.

Ask the children if they can recall examples of climates and weather affecting other people in the world. For example, they may remember television pictures of hurricanes in the southern USA. Ask them to maintain a watch for news of such events and to collect newspaper reports. Plot these events on a world map in the classroom. Discuss how climates affect people's lives and their livelihoods.

Collect newspaper and magazine reports on climatic change.

## Further activities
Use reference books to find out the causes of climatic change. Research climate in the past, using history and science books, for example, frost fairs on the Thames in the seventeenth century, evidence of the Ice Age, and ideas about how climatic change may have caused the extinction of dinosaurs.

# 3. Clean air, dirty air

## Foundation subject links
Science, technology, geography.

## Age range
Seven to eleven.

## Group size
Four to eight.

## What you need
Pictures of air pollution (London smogs in the past, Tokyo police wearing gauze masks, industrial sites or power stations), a cyclist's mask or a do-it-youself disposable mask, clean jars, filter papers, funnels.

### What to do

Use the photographs as a stimulus for a discussion on how air can be polluted. Ask children to list possible sources of pollutants in the air. Where might the air be the most polluted?

Ask a child or children to wear a disposable mask for a few hours. This could be done in several locations: on an outing in the streets, in the countryside, around the school. Use a new filter on each occasion and keep them for comparison in plastic bags. Which air seemed the least clean? Was the test fair?

Rain can remove some impurities from the air (dust and particles, soluble gases). Ask the children to collect rainwater in clean jars. It may look clean, but if it is filtered through absorbent paper, some impurities will be separated out and may be clearly visible.

### Further activity

Look at the possible effects of wind on air pollution.

## 4. Pedestrian crossing

### Foundation subject links

Technology, geography.

### Age range

Five to eleven, with appropriate modifications.

### Group size

The whole class and small groups.

### What you need

A large-scale map of your area, with only one or two roads for younger children (the Ordnance Survey 1:1,250 maps are best for this); card, paints, paper, pencils.

### What to do

Ask the children to make the environment safer by planning safer pedestrian crossings and access. Look at the local roads

with the class. Ask them to look for places where it might be unsafe for pedestrians.

The children should find these locations on the local map. What can be done to make the area safer? Can the pedestrians be kept from the traffic? Or can they be directed to a safe place to cross?

Ask groups to select an area for their plans and then to design a crossing sign to go with it. They could poll local people to find out their views and conduct tests to see which signs seem the most visible and the most effective.

### Further activity

Invite the local road safety officer to school to look at the proposals and to offer comments on their locations and designs.

## 5. Calming the traffic

### Foundation subject links

Geography, technology.

### Age range

Seven to eleven.

### Group size
Groups of four to six.

### What you need
Paper, pencils, a watch with a second hand or stop-watch; large-scale maps and a camera may be useful; parent drivers; a road safety officer or a local police officer.

### What to do
Environmental hazards for children often include traffic which moves too fast through residential areas and near schools. Can the children devise some alternative ways to slow down traffic in their local streets?

Look at the speed at which traffic moves in the local streets. A group could time vehicles over a measured distance and calculate average speeds. Look also for ways in which the traffic can be slowed down, for example, 'speed humps', speed limit signs, narrow restrictions on streets, central reservations and bollards.

In class, ask groups if they can think of other ways that the traffic on the roads they have observed could be slowed down. They could devise plans of the road showing their proposed road markings and traffic lanes. Would they need signs to warn the traffic?

Invite some parent drivers into school to look at the proposals and to make suggestions.

### Further activity
A road safety officer or a local police officer may be able to offer advice, suggestions and comment on the children's proposals.

## 6. Keeping it warm

### Foundation subject links
Science, technology.

### Age range
Seven to eleven.

### Group size
Three to five.

### What you need
Ice cubes and a thermos of hot water – not boiling; a set of similar-sized mugs or plastic cups or similar-sized clean tin cans; thermometers; watches; paper; pencils; a variety of possible insulating materials such as corrugated cardboard, an old blanket, aluminium foil; black and white paint; silver paper.

### What to do
Discuss energy conservation with the class. Emphasise that if we are concerned about the environmental consequences of using up energy supplies, we need to ensure that what energy we do use is not wasted. We heat up rooms in winter: how can we make sure that this heat is not lost too easily?

The hot water can represent the heat in a room. Pour it into a container and it will cool

down. Ask the children which is better for energy conservation: for it to cool down quickly or slowly?

Ask the children to fill a container with hot water and measure the temperature over several minutes to find out how quickly it cools down. They could use a watch to record the temperature at regular intervals. What can they do to slow down the heat loss? Ask the children to try out different lagging materials. Which do they predict will be the most effective? Does the amount of material used have any effect? How much is cooling slowed down? Does putting the container in different places have an effect, for example, if it is placed in a draught?

When the children have found out the best way to stop the water cooling, ask them how they could use the information they have discovered to keep rooms and houses warm. What kind of insulation would be needed and where should it be used?

Keeping things cool also uses energy. Can the children predict the best way to keep things cool? Some children may suggest the opposite to what they have found (seeing hot and cold as 'opposites' rather than simple gradients in temperature). Ask them to experiment and discover the requirements for keeping things cool.

## Further activity

The children could experiment with painting the containers different colours, to see if the colour of the container affects the loss of temperature; black and white or silver give the sharpest differences.

# 7. Soil types

## Foundation subject links
Geography, science.

## Age range
Five to eleven, with appropriate variations.

## Group size
Four to six.

## What you need
Different types of soil – sand, garden clay, gravel, humus or peat; composts and fertilisers; seedlings; jam-jars; water; plastic drinks bottles; scissors; cotton wool.

## What to do
Ask the children to put some samples of local soil in jam jars with some water. They should then shake them up and let the different layers settle: stones to the bottom, then coarse sand, fine sand, clay and organic matter floating on top. Show the children how garden soil is generally a mixture of the different types of materials. How long does the muddy water take to settle?

Ask the children to look at the sand and clay samples. What kind of soil will they form? Pour water on them and let them dry out so that the children can see that sand lets the water through but clay does not. Ask them to describe the differences between sand and clay.

Help the children mix up different kinds of soil (make your garden samples with more clay, more sand or with more peat). They should then put the soils in pots made by cutting the tops off old plastic water bottles, inverting the necks over the bases, and plugging the opening with cotton wool. This allows children to see the effects of watering the soils. They can now plant seedlings in each type of soil. Ask them to keep a record of how the plants develop. Which soils need the most water? Which soils become water logged?

## Further activity
Ask the children to collect soil samples from several locations and compare them. They could try adding various composts and fertilisers to the soils and compare the plants grown in them.

# 8. Acid rain

### Foundation subject links
Science, geography.

### Age range
Nine to eleven.

### Group size
Three to five.

### What you need
Litmus indicator paper, clean jars for collecting rainfall.

## What to do
Ask the children to collect rain and test it with litmus to see whether it is acidic or not. If the paper turns red, it is acidic. Blue indicates alkalinity. They should then compare the results with tap water and bottled water (the latter often has the acidity level stated on the label). Water that is neither acidic nor alkaline has a pH value of 7 and leaves the litmus paper purple.

Ask the children to test rain collected at different times. They could try to find out if the direction of the wind has any effect on the acidity.

## Further activity
The children could correspond with other schools in the United Kingdom or abroad about acid rain in their localities. They might even exchange samples of water for testing.

# 9. Erosion survey

### Foundation subject links
Geography, technology.

### Age range
Five to eleven, with appropriate modifications.

### Group size
The whole class, divided into smaller groups for parts of the activity.

### What you need
A visit to the coast, hilly or mountainous country with rivers or a slow-flowing river; cameras, clipboards, paper and pencils to collect data; cloth or muslin, clay, coarse and fine sand, hose-pipes, photocopiable pages 180 and 181.

### What to do
The natural shape of the environment is constantly changing. Rivers, sea and wind are eroding parts of the landscape, moving particles over distances and depositing them elsewhere. It is important to focus children's attentions on the idea of slow and gradual change before the visit as the process of erosion is not always easy to see. Signs of human activity to prevent erosion will often be more visible.

Depending on the site visited, look for the following signs.

• At the seaside, you might see sand piled against groynes and breakwaters; areas of fine sand, coarse sand and pebbles; sand dunes showing depositions and cliffs showing erosion. If there are pools or small streams draining into the sea at low tide, it will be possible to see erosion and deposition on a small scale.

• On mountains and hillsides, you might see fast-flowing streams (look for small stones being moved for deep-cut valleys); small falls of stones, rock and soil near streams; and evidence of streams being much larger and fast-flowing in times of heavy rain.

• At slow-flowing rivers, you might see sand and silt piled up on the inside corner of bends, and water flowing faster on the outside of the bends, with the river banks showing signs of being worn away.

### Further activity
It is possible to simulate river erosion and deposition in school, by allowing water to flow from a hose over a length of sand in a long waterproof box or in the playground. Use a clay base to prevent the water seeping away underneath and use cloth (muslin or old tights) at the drain to prevent clogging.

Ask the children to use photocopiable pages 180 and 181 to mark in and predict where erosion and deposition will happen in the future, using the three blank spaces to show the changes continuing.

# 10. Looking at mines and quarries

### Foundation subject links
Geography, technology.

### Age range
Seven to eleven.

### Group size
The whole class and small groups.

### What you need
Access to a quarry, disused or in use; bags for collecting samples, labels.

### What to do
Arrange a visit to a quarry. Before the visit, discuss with the class why we need materials from the ground and the relative merits and disadvantages of quarrying and mining (safety, cost, ease of access, depth of materials, environmental concerns). Discuss the need for safety precautions during the visit.

At the site, look for signs of the different types of material, rock or soil in layers, and for how long it has been extracted. If the quarry is still in use, arrange to talk to site managers or other workers about the processes involved.

Discuss with the class the environmental impact of the quarry. Does it represent an eyesore? How much more material might there be in the hillside? Could it all be extracted? Should disused quarries be filled in with rubbish and covered with topsoil?

### Further activities
The children could collect and classify samples; investigate other materials that are extracted from the ground, and find out about the different technologies and machinery that are needed.

# 11. River pollution

### Foundation subject links
Geography, technology.

### Age range
Seven to eleven (with adaptations for younger children).

### Group size
The whole class.

### What you need
Clipboards, paper, pencils, a camera, jam-jars, disposable rubber gloves, plastic bags, filters and filter paper, addresses of water companies, envelopes and stamps.

### What to do
In this activity, the children will investigate a length of river. Ideally, this could be a project involving several outings to different parts of a river, but a single visit could produce plenty of material.

Ask the children to look for signs of pollution in the river. This could be rubbish floating in the stream which they could classify (bits of sweet paper and cigarette packets, or rubbish from a more regular and perhaps industrial source). It could be pollutants causing the water to foam, to discolour, or to leave deposits on the bank.

Tell the children to use the disposable gloves when collecting samples of water. They should filter the water and look at the deposits left on the paper.

Is the pollution constant along the length of the river being studied?

Are there signs of plant or animal life in the river? Do they appear to have been affected? Ask the children to take photographs as evidence of their findings.

Encourage the children to talk with local people (such as anglers) about changes that they have noticed.

### Further activity
The children could write to the water companies for information about the pollution in the rivers. They should send them accounts of what they have seen and found.

# 12. Water, water, everywhere...

### Foundation subject links
Geography.

### Age range
Nine to eleven.

### Group size
Four to eight.

### What you need
Landranger series maps of the local area (Ordnance Survey 1:50,000); graph paper, pencils, a home-made rain gauge.

### What to do
Ask each group to locate the school on the map and to

identify local landmarks that they know. Then ask them to find all the signs of water that they can in the area. You may want to limit this to within a particular radius of the school (say, 10 miles [15km] –12 inches [30cm] on the map); or you may let them use the entire map. All water is shown in blue. Ask them to list and where possible classify the types of water (rivers, canals, reservoirs, sea, lakes). Do they know any of them? Could a visit be made to some?

How does water reach these locations? How is it replenished? The children could draw local water cycles showing the particular features in the area.

Ask the children to consider how people use the different areas of water. Which ones could be used for drinking, farming, transportation, for industry or for flushing away refuse? Can they see any indications of these uses on the map?

## Further activity
The children could measure rainfall over a period of several weeks, using a home-made rain gauge to record daily levels and plot this on a graph. Is the amount more or less than the children expected? Where does this rain go?

# 13. ...and not a drop to drink

## Foundation subject links
Science, technology.

## Age range
Seven to eleven.

## Group size
Four to six.

## What you need
Various types of dirty water (with mud, washing-up liquid, oil, paint); plastic drinks bottles, newspaper, blotting paper, cotton wool, gravel, sand, clean jars, information from water companies; books about water supply in other countries.

## What to do
Tell the children that they are to devise filtering systems to remove some of the impurities from water. Explain to them that this is simply an experiment to make the water appear clean. Children should be cautioned against tasting the results!

The effectiveness of different filtering materials can be compared. Are some materials more effective with certain pollutants? Do some get used up or clogged up? Which are faster?

Visit a water filtration plant in the area or write to the local water company for information, to see how drinking water is purified.

Ask the class how pure they think water has to be before it is fit to drink. Why do some people buy bottled water? Is there a difference in taste? Can the children devise tests to see if this is so?

### Further activity

The children could investigate water supply in other parts of the world. What can happen when supplies of drinking water are not regular, are not piped or are at some distance from where people live?

## 14. Using water

### Foundation subject links

Technology, mathematics.

### Age range

Seven to eleven.

### Group size

Groups of four to six and individuals.

### What you need

Co-operative parents, paper, pencils, measuring bottles/containers (5-litre size).

### What to do

Ask the groups to estimate how much water each of them (or their households) use in a week. They will need to make a number of measurements of particular uses of water.
• Lavatory cisterns hold about 10 litres (it is sometimes possible to measure this by removing the cistern lid, using the flush and then holding the ballcock up while the cistern is filled from a bucket of measured water).
• Bath and washing-up water can be measured by filling the bath or washing-up bowl with cold water from a measuring bottle/container, until the usual level is reached.
• Shower water can be measured by taking a shower as usual, but with the plug in, and then measuring the water as it is removed from the bath with a container. Water used for tooth-cleaning can be measured in the same way.

• Dishwashers and washing machines are harder to calculate. Children could write to the manufacturers or try to make some estimates. It takes on average 20 litres to fill a washing machine, but each programme requires several fills and the number of these depends on the cycle selected.
• Water used in cooking and in drinking can be measured in a similar way.

Once the children know the volume of water used for each activity, they then need to monitor how many of each of the activities are carried out each week. From this they should be able to calculate the total water consumption for each household.

Does water consumption vary from one household to another? Is consumption level related to the number of people in the household?

### Further activity

Not all water enters the house through the taps! The children could make estimates of the amount of water brought in as constituents of food and drink.

Ask the children to investigate ideas for metering water in the same way that electricity and gas are metered. Do the children think this would bring consumption down very much?

# 15. An energy audit

### Foundation subject links
Science, technology, mathematics.

### Age range
Nine to eleven.

### Group size
Four to six.

### What you need
Co-operative parents, paper, pencils, photocopiable page 182.

### What to do
Ask the children to find out how much energy is used in their homes and what it is used for. As in the previous activity, this will require first measuring consumption rates for individual activities and then counting up the number of times each activity occurs in the course of a week.

Rates of use are fairly easily established for gas and electricity consumption. Parents will have to assist in reading the meters for the increases in electricity or gas consumption which occur when particular machines are turned on for a short period of time.

Consumption of oil, paraffin or solid fuel is not so easy to calculate for particular activities.

The children should use photocopiable page 182 to collect all the findings. Discuss these. Can the children work out the costs of various types of energy? Are they surprised at how much is used in some activities? Can they suggest ways of making energy consumption lower?

### Further activity
The children could find out how much consumption rates change over the seasons.

# 16. Fossil fuels

### Foundation subject links
Science, technology, geography.

### Age range
Seven to eleven.

### Group size
Four to six.

### What you need
Books about fossil fuels; paper, pens, envelopes, addresses of fuel suppliers.

### What to do
The three principal fossil fuels are coal, gas and oil. Many children will be more familiar with oil and gas than with coal.

Ask groups to list the different uses of coal, gas and oil. Which fuel do they use at home in a direct form? Which do they use indirectly? (You may want to remind them that about three-quarters of our electric power is generated from fossil fuels.)

Different members of the group could then do the following:
• list the advantages and disadvantages of each fuel (ease and safety of extraction, ease of transport, dangers);
• find out where each type of fuel comes from (UK or abroad);
• investigate how each type of fuel is extracted and transported.

Ask the class to consider the limits of fossil fuels. Will it matter if they are totally used up in the future? What alternatives are there?

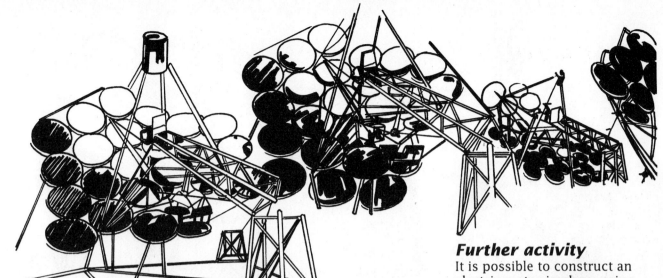

### Further activity
The children could write to various fuel suppliers (British Coal, oil companies, gas companies) for information about their products, and compare their claims.

## 17. Renewable resources

### Foundation subject links
Technology, science.

### Age range
Seven to eleven.

### Group size
Four to six.

### What you need
Junk materials – plastic, card, dowel; LEGO Technic, solar calculator, solar clock, materials to make an electric motor.

### What to do
Discuss the problems associated with using non-renewable fossil fuels (see Activity 16). What suggestions can the children make for other sources of energy?

Some alternative forms of energy have been in use for a long time, for example, windmills and water mills. Tidal power and solar energy have only been used for generating power for a much shorter period. Can the children make devices that will collect some of these forms of energy and turn them into power? Most activities attempted will be for water and wind power. Tidal power is quite difficult to capture and so it is probably best to try to get some kind of rotation as a result. Rotating movement can be used directly to drive machinery (LEGO Technic) or to generate electric power.

Which group can produce the most efficient/fastest energy device or the device using the least materials? Why is this important? Look at solar energy devices on the calculator and the clock.

Ask the class to discuss the comparative advantages of fossil and renewable energy sources.

### Further activity
It is possible to construct an electric motor in class, using long lengths of fine coated wire, magnets, corks, pins and needles (see illustration). If spun around at speed, enough power can be generated to light a small light bulb. Suitable groups, with assistance, could attempt to harness their wind/water mills to an electric motor.

## 18. The nuclear debate

### Foundation subject links
Science, technology, English.

### Age range
Nine to eleven.

### Group size
The whole class (some group work for preparation).

### What you need
A variety of information sources on nuclear energy (from nuclear authorities and environmental groups).

### What to do
Organise a class debate on the positive and negative aspects of nuclear power generation. Groups and individuals will need to brief themselves on

the various issues involved (safety, cost, resource issues, pollution and radiation dangers, storage of waste) and to prepare their points of view.

You may like to organise the debate formally or informally. Take a vote at the end to see who is in favour of nuclear power.

### Further activity
Invite visitors from your various information sources to visit the school and discuss the issues with the children.

## 19. Population change

### Foundation subject links
Science, mathematics, geography.

### Age range
Seven to eleven.

### Group size
Three to six.

### What you need
Photocopiable page 183, pencils, calculators.

### What to do
Discuss problems of world population growth with the class (see pages 104 to 105). You may wish to point out that families in this country were much larger in the past than the present average.

Photocopiable page 183 is a mathematical simulation that shows how the world population will continue to rise. It is based on 100 people, representing all the people of the world today. Each vertical column is used to show the number of people in ten-year intervals. The first year's numbers are shown, which approximately represent the distribution of the age ranges in the world today. Each horizontal column shows the number of people in a particular age range. This means that the number of those aged 0-10 in this year's column will become the number of people in the 11-20 year old column in ten year's time.

The simulation makes a number of assumptions that you can discuss with the class:
• all children are born to people aged between 21 and 30;
• all people have children;
• half the people aged 51-60 die before reaching the 61-70 column (truer worldwide than for the United Kingdom);
• a further half of those aged 61-70 die before reaching the 71-80 column;
• nobody survives beyond 80;
• there are no deaths other than these.

The number to be put into the 0-10 column for each year depends on the number of adults aged 21-30 in the same year. If every couple has two children, then the number is the same. If they have three

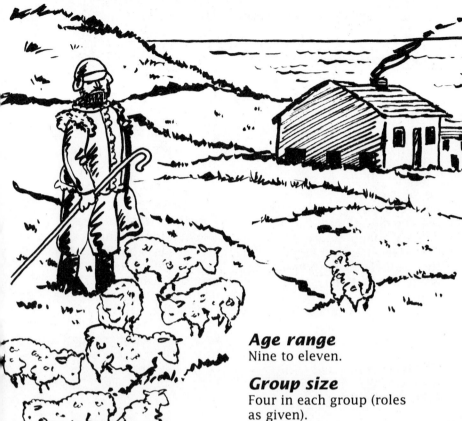

children, then the number is half as much again, and so on.

You could give different groups of children different average family sizes: one, two, three or four children per family.

When the numbers for each age have been calculated, the total 'population for the world' can be worked out.

Discuss how the population rises, even if initially there is only one child per couple. What are the implications for global resources?

# 20. Farming life

## Foundation subject links
Geography, English.

## Age range
Nine to eleven.

## Group size
Four in each group (roles as given).

## What you need
Photocopiable pages 184 and 187 (one set per group); photocopiable pages 185 and 186 (two to three sets per class).

## What to do
This activity is designed to help children see how other societies view their environment. The children are asked to role-play individuals in a peasant economy.

Use the four role cards on photocopiable page 184. Photocopiable page 187 is a map that shows the area. Each group will need one of these.

Explain to the groups that they are members of a farming community, far away from cities and towns. It could be a croft in the Scottish Isles, or somewhere on the African savannah or a settlement in the rural American colonies – the problems are much the same. The inhabitants have to make certain decisions about their way of life and accept what consequences follow.

Outline the situation to all the class. They are farming families that get nearly all their food from their own crops and livestock. The essential outcome is to survive and not to take any action that may threaten that. They can make much of their clothes from animal products. They only sell a few particular crops (not ones that they eat themselves) once a year to a trader, who sells them oil for lighting, sugar, salt and a few other things that they cannot produce for themselves.

Each group should study their own role cards and make a group decision about what crops to plant and animals to keep the next year. They write down their decisions.

They then are dealt or choose a situation card (see photocopiable page 185). This requires them to make a further decision. When they have made their choice, they should be given a second slip (photocopiable page 186) that tells them of the consequence of their decision. They can then modify their plans, if they wish. You could allow the groups to draw another situation card if you wish and to continue the game.

After the simulation, bring the class together to discuss the problems they encountered and how they tried to solve them. How important is the environment to these people? Why? How are their lives different from the children's lives?

# 21. Industrial waste

### Foundation subject links
Technology, geography.

### Age range
Seven to eleven.

### Group size
The whole class and small groups.

### What you need
A camera, a tape recorder, paper, pencils.

### What to do
Visit a small local manufacturer who produces some industrial waste. This could be offcuts of materials or chemical waste – the exact nature is not very important. Ask the children to discuss with the manufacturer the processes involved and how the company tries to minimise waste production.

How much waste is produced? How does the company dispose of it? How much does it cost to dispose of the waste? What are the problems connected with disposal? Was it always got rid of in this way?

With permission, take photographs of the production process and particularly of the waste disposal.

If the waste is safe, ask if the children can think of some alternative uses for the material. Ask if they can take samples back to school to experiment with (some classes have made toys, musical instruments or science kits from industrial waste collected in this way).

### Further activities
The children might like to make a class book on waste disposal from the manufacturing unit. They might also want to explore alternative methods of disposal or recycling the waste. Invite the manufacturer to school to discuss the children's proposals with them.

# 22. Technology challenge

### Foundation subject links
Technology, geography.

### Age range
Seven to eleven.

### Group size
Four to six.

### What you need
Scrap materials for model making.

### What to do
This activity explores ideas of 'appropriate' or 'intermediate' technology. Many modern technological processes are inappropriate for developing societies: they are too expensive, too complex to maintain and require too sophisticated a level of maintenance. The challenge is to devise tools that are appropriate (cheap, reliable, long-lasting and easy to use).

Offer each group a different challenge:
• a tool for hoeing weeds out of the soil and breaking up lumps of clay;
• a toy for a seven-year-old;
• a system for recording crop planting and production, field by field;
• a machine for washing clothes;
• an irrigation scheme that does not require concrete dams.

Discuss the design proposal and, where appropriate, ask groups to make models or prototypes. Compare the various results proposed. Offer criticisms if you think that the designs fail to meet the criteria of cheapness, reliability and simplicity.

## 23. Waste-bin survey

### Foundation subject links
Technology, science, mathematics.

### Age range
Five to nine.

### Group size
Four to six.

### What you need
Paper, pencils, disposable gloves, a school equipment catalogue.

### What to do
Towards the end of the afternoon, set a group to sort through the day's class rubbish wearing disposable gloves. The children could either work only on the material in the bin or pick up rubbish left on the floor as well. Ask them first to list the objects found and then to sort them into piles (used paper, unused paper, whole sheets, other materials and so on).

What is the cost of the material being thrown out? Use the catalogues to calculate its value. If the floor-clearing activity is followed, the children could arrive at surprisingly large sums – normally, of course, objects such as dropped scissors are put away, rather than thrown out!

The children could calculate the total lost in a week from the class and then assume that each class in the school throws

out the same. What is the total value of the waste thrown out in a year? How does this compare with the school's budget allocation for materials?

What waste materials could be reused? Can waste paper be recycled – clean bits trimmed and used, used bits perhaps turned into papier mâché, or used in other kinds of modelling?

Ask the groups to talk with the headteacher about the costs of school materials and how much is wasted, and with the caretaker about the way she or he deals with the rubbish.

# 24. Litter and the environment

## Foundation subject links
Geography, English.

## Age range
Seven to nine.

## Group size
The whole class and groups of two to four.

## What you need
Paper, clipboards, pencils, materials for making signs and posters.

## What to do
Ask the children to draw plans of the school playground, marking entrances and corridors. One group could do this and then make copies for the others.

Divide up the total area of the playground and corridors into small areas. These need to be easily identifiable and to cover all the 'public' areas of the school. Ideally, each area would be of an equal size, but this may not always be practicable.

Each group should be allocated a number of small areas. Their task is to survey the amount and types of litter in each area. They should be as precise as possible.

The whole class should then map the 'litter density' of the school. Colour in the worst areas red, the next orange, then yellow and blue for the most litter-free areas. Is there a pattern of litter? Where are the worst areas? What could be done there?

Ask the children to consider the kinds of litter. Which are the most common items? Why are they left as litter?

The whole class could then discuss the findings with the school caretaker and the cleaners. Have they got any suggestions?

Encourage the class to mount a school anti-litter campaign. Groups or individual children could design and make signs and posters. Hold an assembly to publicise the survey and the campaign.

### Further activity
Conduct another survey of the school after a few days. Has there been an improvement? Do a further survey a fortnight later: were the improvements permanent?

# 25. Wildlife reserve

### Foundation subject links
Science, geography.

### Age range
Five to eleven.

### Group size
The whole class, with specific smaller groups in a rota over the period; the whole school will need to be involved.

### What you need
Some spare ground near the school or in the school grounds, a camera, paper, pencils.

### What to do
Construct a school wildlife reserve. You will need an area at least three metres by three metres. Discuss with the class the kinds of wildlife that are found in the area (minibeasts, butterflies, birds). What do they need in the way of an environment?

Create a variety of secure places in the wildlife reserve (old paving stones, old logs and tree stumps, possibly a shallow pool, areas of shade and sunlight). It is important to construct pathways, which children can follow without disturbing the soil or plants. Leave the wildlife reserve alone as far as possible, watering if necessary in dry patches.

Ask the children to take photographs of the wildlife reserve at regular intervals through the year. A series of photographs from the same vantage point can be interesting, but it is also useful to photograph particular items.

The children might also like to draw and plot the changes that occur as the garden establishes itself. There will often be phases where one particular plant or insect appears to predominate and then be succeeded by another, as the plot settles down to become stable. Discuss the changes with the children.

# 26. Paper recycling

### Foundation subject links
Technology.

### Age range
Five to eleven, with appropriate modifications.

### Group size
Up to six.

### What you need
Used paper in a fairly clean condition, a bowl, a spoon, a food mixer, squares of fine net (50cm × 50cm) fixed over a wooden frame, water, old newspapers.

### What to do
This activity shows how paper can be recycled and raises several problems for discussion associated with this.

The used paper needs to be torn into small pieces – preferably less than a square centimetre. It should then be left to soak in water and stirred regularly until the fibres disentangle (as for papier mâché). Alternatively, small quantities can be pulverised with water in the food mixer.

When the paper has been broken down into fibres, ask the children to stir the mixture well. They should then either immerse the frame with the netting into the mix and raise it to create a layer of fibres, or pour a cup of the mixture over the netting placed on an old newspaper. The former gives a more even sheet of material; the latter may allow more control over the thickness.

Allow the bulk of the water to drain away, so that the fibres begin to lock together. The children can then peel off the layer and place it to dry. If the layer is very thin, it may help to begin the drying process on the netting.

Ask the groups to examine the paper they have made and to comment on its quality (thickness, colour, smoothness, etc.). Can the children think of any possible uses it might have? What could be done to improve the quality? Colouring matter can be added, or the mixture could be bleached (do *not* do this in class: the process needs great care!), but these processes may not be helpful in protecting the environment.

### Further activity
Encourage the children to look out for examples of recycled paper in everyday use.

# CHAPTER 5

# Education for citizenship

Citizenship is not an area which has featured in any description of the primary curriculum before. There have been various studies made of the development of young children's political awareness and understanding, but these have not generally been linked to curriculum. Citizenship is concerned with the relationships between the individual and society. As with the other cross-curricular themes, its central concern is to empower young people to participate effectively in social groupings and not simply 'know about' them.

All children take part in social activities and are actively learning about the ways in which these groups operate. Many children have a genuine interest in how the country is organised, for example, what the laws are, how they are made, and in elections. Children also learn from the reactions of teachers and other adults that many of these issues are sensitive ones. Education for citizenship can in this sense be regarded as a consolidation of existing social learning. There is an important distinction to be made between political education and political indoctrination. Some teachers have become so cautious that many children have learned to avoid asking questions about citizenship. However, while there are important legal restrictions on political education, education for citizenship is now a cross-curricular theme that must be included as part of a broad and balanced curriculum, and so the situation must change.

There are various reasons for including education for citizenship in the primary curriculum. Some of the government's concerns are revealed in the National Curriculum Council's reference to the 'duties, responsibilities and rights of citizenship' in Curriculum Guidance 8: Education for Citizenship (1990). The emphasis on 'duties' perhaps betrays a concern that young people themselves are more concerned with their rights. However, young people need to be empowered, so that they can effectively participate in social and political life rather than passively accept decisions made by others.

Education for citizenship is important and necessary for a healthy society. As the Secretary of State for Education and Science put it in a speech to the National Conference of the Commission on Citizenship in Schools in 1990: '...unless citizenship forms a part of what schools seek to convey to their pupils, the aim [of a broad and balanced curriculum] as set out in the [Education Reform] Act will not be achieved.'

# BACKGROUND

At first sight, education for citizenship might appear to be even more alien to the young child than economic and industrial understanding. At least, it might be argued, children see and take part in economic transactions in shops, handle money and are consumers; but politics, remote from their direct experience, is an area in which they cannot participate until they are old enough to vote. However, others would argue that children are concerned about social order, social justice and morality; and that while the formal structures of national (and even local) government may be remote from their experience, these questions do arise within communities of which children have direct experience (family, school, friendship groups, neighbourhood and so on). It is also argued that mass communications now make indirect experiences more vivid and less remote, and young children have a much greater exposure to world political activity such as the fall of the Berlin Wall, the Gulf War or famine in Africa. The greater incidence of migration in the modern world also makes it much more likely that some children will have had direct experience of such an event.

We can approach education for citizenship with two distinct questions in mind:
• What are the questions and issues that interest young children?
• What does society need young people to know?

While the first question might appear to limit children to an agenda that they define for themselves, the second question also presents problems, in that different individuals and groups will have different notions of what 'society' is and what it needs.

In the National Curriculum Council's document *Curriculum Guidance 8* (1990) we are told that society's needs provide both the fundamental rationale for education for citizenship and a definition of the agenda to be covered: '...education for citizenship develops the knowledge, skills and attitudes necessary for exploring, making informed decisions about and exercising responsibilities and rights in a democratic society.'

The implicit rationale for education for citizenship in this document is the need to ensure that future electors know their place within the existing system and understand their duties to maintain the system. However, it is open to teachers to adopt wider perspectives: one could include consideration of alternative views of society, for example; or begin by looking at the specific areas that are of concern to children.

## Children's perspectives

Research shows that children have a number of questions about political systems.
• Why are some people more powerful than others? What can those with power properly ask others to do?
• Why do we have rules? Where do they come from? What happens if we do not follow them? Can they be changed?
• Is it the job of the police force to make sure that the law is obeyed? Why do we have courts as well? What are the differences?
• Why are things (money, food, material goods) not shared equally or at least more equitably? Why does the world of grown-ups often appear so unfair?
• What happens (and what ought to happen) when an individual disagrees with a group or community decision? How far can or should they go in their disagreement?
• Why do people work together and collaborate to achieve their goals? What does this cost in terms of loss of individual goals?
• Why do groups of people have different goals? Why can't different goals always be reconciled?
• Are there rights that everyone has? Why? Where do they come from? Why doesn't everyone have them?
• Why do people vote? What do they vote for? Why can't

most people vote for or against the Prime Minister? Can the Queen tell the Prime Minister what to do? Who is really 'in charge'?

If we consider the sort of information and stories that young children are exposed to, it is quite understandable why these questions arise. A lot of children's literature presents images of royal authority that conflict with contemporary experience of a constitutional monarchy. Adults are often presented as though their rights to 'be in charge' result solely from their age and some children consequently think that the older one gets, the more powerful one becomes. Some television series present stories in which the police, or even private individuals, are seen to be enforcing justice in defiance of the law; while some news reports suggest that the police on occasion conspire to frustrate justice. It is not surprising that children receive conflicting and confusing messages about how the world operates.

## The legal position

Education for citizenship has been included in England and Wales by the National Curriculum Council in its

definition of 'the whole curriculum' (Education Reform Act, 1988). But there is other legislation governing this area: the Education (No 2) Act (1986) has two clauses in particular. The local education authority, the governing body and the headteacher shall:
• '...forbid the pursuit of partisan political activities by...junior pupils; and the promotion of partisan political views in the teaching of any subject in the school.'
(Section 44)
• '...secure that where political issues are brought to the attention of pupils (...) they are offered a balanced presentation of opposing views.' (Section 45)

In terms of teacher practice, it is clear that the 1986 Act permits political education in primary schools, within the constraints of not being overtly biased. Indeed, the whole curriculum required by the 1988 Act needs education for citizenship to be included for all children.

## Participation and enactive learning

Traditional approaches to secondary subjects such as civics were largely descriptive of the structures and forms of various political institutions. Arguably, even with older pupils, this was a highly inappropriate way to develop understanding of how political systems work. The reasons advanced from across the political spectrum for education for citizenship today, are to encourage active participation in the system so that future generations do not succumb to the alternatives of alienation, apathy or anarchy. The stress in schools (and particularly in primary schools) should be on exploration, participation and discussion, so that children develop understanding, attitudes and skills that will enable them to take an appropriate part in social/public life, now and in the future. Informed decisions about whether and how to take part in political society (including decisions about trying to change that society), and exercising rights and responsibilities in society follow from a programme of education for citizenship.

### Knowledge

Participation and enactive learning is education which enables children to do things effectively, not just to know things. Some knowledge is necessary, but knowledge acquired within the context of skills of participation, not knowledge acquired in isolation. The framework of knowledge suggested in the National Curriculum Council's *Curriculum Guidance 8* (1990) develops three main strands:

*1. The nature of community*
• the variety of communities to which people simultaneously belong – family, school, local, national, European and worldwide;
• how communities combine stability with change;
• how communities are organised and the importance of rules and laws;
• how communities reconcile the needs of individuals with those of society.

*2. Roles and relationships in a democratic society*
• the nature of co-operation and competition between individuals, groups and communities;
• similarities and differences between individuals, groups and communities – diversity and interdependence;
• the experience and opportunities of people in different roles and communities.

*3. The nature and basis of duties, responsibilities and rights*
• the role of custom and law in prescribing duties, responsibilities and rights;
• fairness, justice and moral responsibility.

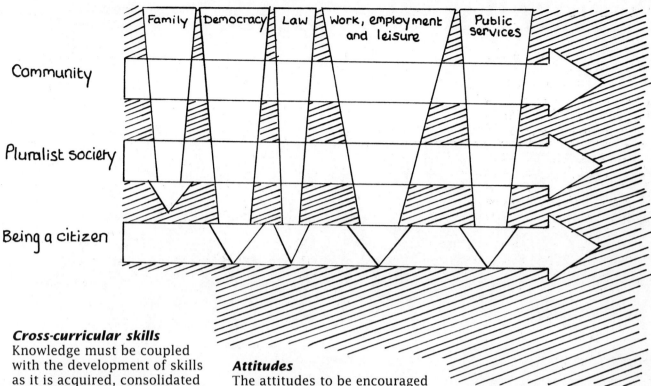

Figure 1

## Cross-curricular skills

Knowledge must be coupled with the development of skills as it is acquired, consolidated and extended through the growth of these skills. Most of the cross-curricular skills listed in the National Curriculum Council's *Curriculum Guidance 3: The Whole Curriculum* (1990) provide a useful way to categorise these skills:
*1. Communication skills*
• arguing a case clearly and concisely;
• detecting opinion, bias and omission in evidence.
*2. Numeracy skills*
• collecting, classifying and evaluating data;
• interpreting statistics and working out probabilities.
*3. Problem-solving skills*
• recognising and defining the nature of a problem;
• making choices in the light of available evidence.
*4. Personal and social skills*
• working with others;
• exercising democratic responsibilities and rights (for example, participating in class councils or school elections).

## Attitudes

The attitudes to be encouraged in education for citizenship are less easy to define, because any list of attitudes needs to include only those which allow respect for, justice and respect for others, and not those which define particular courses of action. A list might include:
• independence of thought on social and moral issues;
• an enterprising and persistent approach to tasks and challenges;
• a sense of fair play, including respect for the processes of law and the rights of others;
• respect for different ways of life, beliefs, opinions and ideas;
• a willingness to respect the legitimate interests of others;
• a respect for rational argument and non-violent ways of resolving conflict;
• a constructive interest in community affairs;
• an active concern for human rights;
• appreciation of the paramount importance of democratic decision-making.

## The basic components of a programme for citizen education

There are three broad areas that cover the field of citizenship (see the horizontal bands in Figure 1):
• the nature of a community;
• roles and relationships within a pluralist society;
• the rights and duties of a citizen.

These broad areas can be seen in five everyday contexts for citizenship (see the vertical bands in Figure 1):
• the family;
• democracy;
• law and the citizen;
• work, employment, leisure;
• public services.

### The nature of community

This area is concerned with how individuals and groups relate together to form communities. Membership of communities may be formal or informal, but it brings with it rights and duties towards others in the community. Communities offer stability, but are nearly always changing and adapting.

Within the theme of community, children could look at different kinds of communities: families (social), workplaces (economic), local authorities (political); at the different roles within communities, and the rights and duties that go with them;

and at power, influence and authority within communities. They could examine how individual and group needs are met, and the benefits and disadvantages that community membership entails.

Infant children could, for example, list all the groups that they belong to and discuss how large each group is. What are the special characteristics of each group? What do the groups do? The children could find out about people with particular jobs or duties within each group.

Older children could look at wider groups and communities of which they are members, for example, a particular region or the European Community. What sort of links are they aware of within these communities? What information, trade and friendship patterns are found within these communities?

### Pluralist society

Modern societies are not homogeneous: they are composed of different groups, with different beliefs, attitudes and customs. Different groups will have different needs and wants. These needs, beliefs and attitudes will often conflict and lead to groups opposing each other. Successful pluralist societies have certain shared value systems which tolerate a variety of cultures and lifestyles, and preserve the rights of individuals and minorities without jeopardising the well-being of majorities.

Modern democracy is not simply a matter of the largest group being able to impose its will on the rest of society. It is concerned with the preservation of the rights of minorities and individuals, and the equality of all citizens. This broad area therefore considers issues of justice, diversity, fairness, cooperation, prejudice and discrimination. Children are aware of such issues at a very early age, and schools can help children articulate and develop ideas. Children need to understand the differences and the interdependence between individuals, groups and society. This needs to be linked to reconciling different perceptions, particularly within the context of Britain as a multilingual, multi-faith, multi-ethnic society. These explorations should not be confined to any legalistic notion of 'citizenship', but also consider, for example, the rights of refugees, visitors and other 'non-citizens' living in Britain, as well as stateless and displaced persons around the world.

Infant children need to begin exploring these issues by looking at different roles in social groups with which they are familiar (families, school, friendship groups), and the similarities and differences between cultures represented in Britain. Where appropriate, the existence and origins of prejudice, and the need to counter discrimination should be explored.

Junior children could look at the languages spoken in the school and the community or the various faiths to be found in the area. Exploration of the varieties of social and cultural groupings can be linked to an examination of the underlying similarities.

Junior children are particularly interested in ideas of fairness and social justice, and should be encouraged to discuss how societies can be fair to minorities and ensure that all citizens are treated equally.

### Being a citizen

Being an effective and active member of a democratic society entails developing and using a complex set of skills. These often grow and progress through adult life, and only the foundations can be laid during the period of statutory education. Central to the concept of citizenship is the idea that the individual is granted particular fundamental rights by society and that, in

return, he or she has certain duties towards society. The British state has always declined to formulate a list of rights (unlike some other modern states), but it is possible to suggest civil, political, social and human rights that are seen as fundamental. Rights are often described as freedoms, for example: freedom of speech that does not incite others; freedom to participate in electoral and other democratic activities; freedom from arbitrary arrest; freedom to meet, associate, marry; and freedom from hunger and homelessness. Other rights include those of access (for example, to justice and law) which, in some societies, may be limited by the individual's ability to pay or social connections. Rights can be

violated (and often are), sometimes by the state itself, and sometimes by groups and individuals, for example, through sexist or racist discrimination. Having such rights involves the citizen in certain duties to society: to respect the rule of law, for example, or to meet financial obligations to the state imposed through taxation. Some kind of balance between rights and duties exists, and it can be argued that there is a point where if rights are threatened or withdrawn, then the individual no longer owes any duties to society.

In infant classes, notions of citizenship can be explored through talking about social behaviour. What are the advantages of sharing or turn-taking? What do individuals have to give up if such a system is to succeed? What are the disadvantages of bullying? Some children will also want to discuss wider notions of human rights, perhaps prompted by television images: rights to freedom from hunger, disease and war.

Junior children can explore ideas of rights and duties in a more detailed and sustained way. For example, role-playing a small society (evolving on a desert island) can lead to detailed discussions as to how this society might be organised. Children at this age can conduct simple investigations of why and how societies differ.

### Family

Families can be a sensitive issue to discuss in school, because there are a wide variety of family types, many of which do not match the rather idealised 'normal' family. It is crucial that teachers – and politicians – do not make assumptions about family life and parenthood that will not accord with the experiences of some children, and that may make them feel inadequate and 'wrong'. Children need to recognise the variety of family types, and to value the relationships that exist in the family and domestic units of which they have experience. The proportion of marriages that end in divorce and the number of children being raised by single parents are now such that in many areas this is more 'normal' than other models of family structure. Sensitive teachers will not wish to make children feel that their home arrangements are inadequate and will be able to openly discuss issues such as separation and divorce when this is appropriate, both with individual children and with larger groups.

Infant children will talk naturally with each other and with adults in the school about their homes, and the adults and older children who live with them and care for them. This can be set in the context

of their physical and emotional growth and development, and of the various kinds of relationships that can exist in a wide variety of family and domestic groups.

Junior children can look in more detail at the variety of family groups that can be found, perhaps through drawing their own family trees. Where appropriate, they could talk to adults (including members of their own family) about changes in family life.

### Democracy

This aspect of citizenship develops the political aspects of being a citizen, so that eventually children will understand the essentials of the political system in this country, and of the part that they will be able to play within it. The skills necessary for eventual participation can be developed through activities in school, for example, ways of making decisions and choices, ways in which opinions can be expressed and attempts made to persuade others to change their views. Sometimes, particularly with older junior children, discussion and role-

play will closely follow adult political processes and issues, particularly when these are matters immediately in the news, for example, at the time of a general election. But in primary schools there will not generally be much discussion or knowledge about formal political systems at a governmental or international level.

Infant children, for example, might decide what is the fairest way to share out tasks in keeping the classroom tidy. How can decisions about this be made? What different ideas are there? How are these expressed? What problems might a rota bring? Questions such as these develop early political skills that will be built on in later education about democratic forms.

Junior children can be involved in more formal decision-making and rule-making events. Listening to other people's views, deciding what to do when opinions differ and reaching

conclusions that are fair to both the majority and the minorities, help develop political skills.

### The citizen and the law

Laws impose a wide range of obligations and duties on citizens, restricting individual freedoms for the sake of wider needs of society; in doing so, they define and limit individual and group rights. Individuals and groups may have different and various moral codes and notions of right and wrong, but the law sets out a common code for all members of society. Children need to know how and why laws are formed. They also need to explore the differences between the making of a law, the policing of society and the enforcement of the law.

Infant children may discuss issues of safety and care. What sorts of things protect us from danger? How can we prevent people from harming us?

Junior children may make a more sustained and focused exploration of some aspect of the law, for example, looking at a particular type of behaviour, such as dropping litter, or parking in restricted areas in the school car park. They could try to find out why people behave in such a way, what the law says they should do and consider what alternatives there are to modifying this behaviour.

### Work, employment and leisure

While work, employment and leisure have been covered in economic and industrial understanding (Chapter 2) and careers education and guidance (Chapter 4), the inclusion of these issues under the umbrella of education for citizenship emphasises the political and social contexts of work and employment. The relationship between work and rights of citizenship (are rights forfeited if an individual does not work and is this fair?), and work and duties (what economic duties does a person in employment owe society?), are complex, but have important consequences. Children will need to differentiate between different kinds of work (including voluntary activities), civil rights at work, unemployment and the rights of the unemployed and so on.

Many of the activities discussed in earlier chapters will be useful in developing these ideas. Talking to people who work in a local shop or library, for example, could help younger children develop ideas about work, earning an income and so on. Older children could develop such activities to include exploring the views of people at work, how they are organised and how they relate to each other, as well as the idea of interdependence at work.

### Public services

Children will become increasingly aware of the range of public services which affect their families and themselves, for example, refuse collection, libraries, swimming pools and schools. They should reflect on how these all contribute to the smooth running of the local community and how they are paid for. The level of public services and how they should be provided is again a current political issue, and one which older children may well be aware of and on which they may offer their own views.

Younger children might look at a local service such as a library and find out who uses the library, who works there and the way in which it is organised. Some children may think about how the service is paid for.

Junior children could make more detailed examinations of the changes in the nature and level of public services over the past century.

# ACTIVITIES

## 1. Which groups do we belong to?

### Foundation subject links
Mathematics, English.

### Age range
Five to nine.

### Group size
Small groups of up to six, which could feed into a class discussion.

### What you need
Paper, coloured pencils or felt-tipped pens, adhesive, scissors, large sheets of paper; photocopiable page 188 may also be used.

### What to do
Ask children to think of all the groups they belong to, for example, their family, their class, friends, clubs and teams, residents in the local area, a religious group or a language group.

Ask them to draw themselves, cut out the picture and mount it at the centre of a large piece of paper. Then ask them to draw other members of the group and create sets of people (all of which will include themselves). They should then label the sets. Some sets will be inclusive, others will intersect (see Figure 2). Photocopiable page 188 gives sets of pictures which can be cut out and labelled as needed in order to save time.

Ask children in the group to discuss and compare their sets. How do they belong to a group? Is anyone in charge of a group? Do the groups have any rules about what its members should do or who they should be?

### Further activity
A class discussion on groups may follow. You could discuss different groups that you belong to, bringing in new examples such as professional associations/trade unions, motoring organisations, adult education classes, neighbourhood watch schemes and libraries.

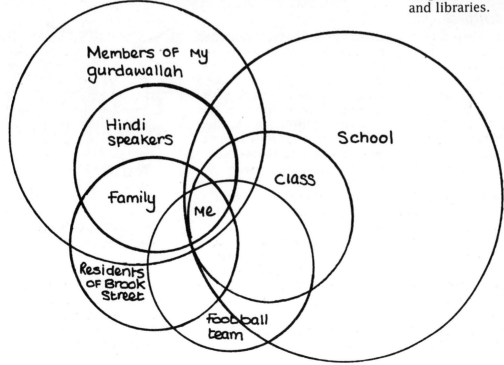

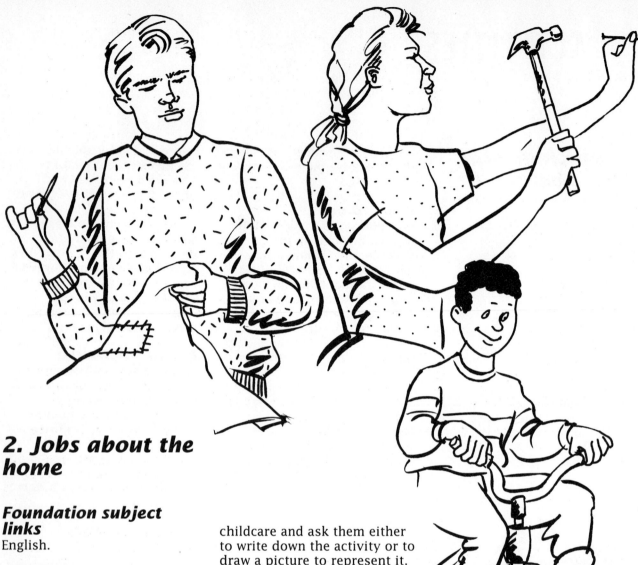

# 2. Jobs about the home

### Foundation subject links
English.

### Age range
Five to nine.

### Group size
Individuals and groups of up to six, which could feed into a class discussion.

### What you need
Paper, coloured pencils or felt-tipped pens, scissors, adhesive.

### What to do
Ask the children to think about all the jobs that there are in the home. Prompt them with ideas such as cleaning, shopping, repairing and childcare and ask them either to write down the activity or to draw a picture to represent it. Then ask each child to make a chart with the names of each member of their family at the top. The children should then cut out and stick down the appropriate task under the name of the person who usually does that job. They may need to draw or write down some activities several times.

Ask small groups of children to discuss differences between their charts. Are some jobs always done by the same members of the family? Why? Are there tasks that can only be done by one particular person? Why?

### Further activity
Talk about families in the past. Encourage the children to talk with older relatives or other people about family life in the 1940s, 1950s or 1960s, and about whether and how things have changed (see 'Changes, changes' on page 145).

# 3. Taking turns

### Foundation subject links
English.

### Age range
Seven to nine.

### Group size
Pairs and sometimes groups of four.

### What you need
No special requirements.

### What to do
Ask each pair to role-play two children in the same family who each want to watch a different programme on the television (there is only one set available). The set is not yet on, but they are arguing about which channel to switch on.

What arguments are used to justify each point of view? What strategies are used to sort out the problem and come to some arrangement? You could set a time limit (when the programmes will start), so that unless an arrangement is made they will both miss out.

Another pair of children could be brought in to the role-play as different members of the family, such as parents or older siblings who do not like the noise of the argument or who have other viewing preferences.

### Further activity
With the whole class, discuss problems of sharing out limited resources (in this case, time). Discuss how systems have to be worked out to share, take turns or otherwise allocate things. Can the children think of things that are not allocated in a fair way?

# 4. Saying 'no' to bullies

### Foundation subject links
English.

### Age range
Five to eleven.

### Group size
Small groups (up to five).

### What you need
Photocopiable page 189.

### What to do
Give each group a slip of paper that outlines a situation in which bullying is about to occur. Photocopiable page 189 contains some possible descriptions. The task of the group is to agree on what is the best course of action to take.

When all the groups have come to their own decision, bring the class together and ask each group in turn to explain their situation and to offer their solutions. It may help to give two groups identical problems, so that responses can be compared.

As the discussion proceeds, ask the children if any of them have been in similar situations or if they have done similar things.

### Further activity
Children could make posters on strategies for confronting bullies and display these around the school. The class could devise an assembly for the rest of the school that highlights the problem and offers possible solutions.

## 5. Caring for each other

### Foundation subject links
English.

### Age range
Five to nine.

### Group size
Four to six.

### What you need
Photocopiable page 190 or a collection of similar photographs, paper.

### What to do
Show the children pictures of people of different ages: a baby, a toddler, a young child, a middle-aged person, a very old person. Ask them to make up stories about the everyday lives of these people (who they might live with and what they might do in a day).

Do people have different needs? What sort of help do different people need? Who gives it to them? When do they need help? Finding responses to these kinds of questions develops children's empathy with other people. A discussion will lead to a recognition of the interdependence between people in a family and in society.

### Further activity
Ask the children to make lists of what sort of help different people need at different times of their lives and who might provide this help. They could draw or paint pictures of these different people.

## 6. Organising the classroom

### Foundation subject links
English.

### Age range
Five to eleven (with appropriate adaptations).

### Group size
The whole class.

### What you need
A class/school timetable, paper, card, pencils, pens, rulers, scissors, a pair of compasses.

## What to do

Discuss with the children all the jobs that there are to be done about the classroom. Ask them to suggest some classroom jobs (tidying up, keeping things in store, handing out materials and equipment).

Make a list of all the classroom jobs. When does each of the jobs need to be done? Ask the children to use the class/school timetable to find out when and how often each task occurs in the week. How many people need to be involved?

Which are the most popular jobs? Which are the jobs that nobody wants to do? What is the fairest and most efficient way to share all these jobs between members of the class? Leaving the tidying up to those children who can do it the most quickly and neatly may lead to a tidy classroom, but might not be fair; and how would the untidy children ever learn to be tidy?

Ask groups of children to make up different kinds of rotas to show who should do which jobs and when they should do them. These rotas could be lists or rotating circles (with windows to show names against particular jobs). Try out some of the rotas with the class.

## Further activity

After a few days or weeks, review the rotas that have been put forward and tried. Do they work as expected? Does everyone feel that they are fair? Is the classroom working smoothly? What modifications need to be made?

# 7. Rules to stay safe

## Foundation subject links

English, physical education.

## Age range

Seven to eleven.

## Group size

Four to six.

## What you need

Paper, coloured pencils or felt-tipped pens, examples of safety rules.

## What to do

While some rules prevent us behaving in particular ways, others are devised as advice to keep us safe. This activity is about the latter kind of rules, for example, non-compulsory codes of conduct for crossing the road or for behaviour in swimming pools.

Talk about laws that are made by Parliament, which we all have to follow, and the difference between these and the rules that we make to keep ourselves safe. Ask the class to think about the difference between what happens when laws are broken and when safety rules are broken.

Ask groups of children to devise safety codes for the following situations:
• in the school corridors,
• at lunchtime,
• on a class trip to the library or swimming baths,
• in the kitchen, at home,
• in the countryside,
• beside a canal or river.

Adapt the situations to meet your own school's particular needs and location.

What are the best ways of expressing the rules so that they are clear and easy to understand and remember? Ask groups to imagine that they are devising an advertising campaign. Which slogans and lists will be most effective?

Draw up lists of rules. Ask the children to illustrate them and try them out on other classes. Mount the best efforts around the school.

### Further activity

Collect other examples of safety rules. Ask groups of children to discuss the safety rules and try to improve on them.

Encourage the children to devise sets of safety rules for using equipment in technology such as knives, saws and glue guns.

## 8. Working for our leisure

### Foundation subject links
English, physical education.

### Age range
Seven to eleven.

### Group size
Six to eight, with some whole-class discussion.

### What you need
No special requirements.

### What to do
Arrange to visit a local sports centre (or somewhere similar) to talk with the people who work there. Different groups could talk with different workers. Can they find out how the community supports and pays for the centre? Discuss with the children how communities organise leisure activities (some are provided by local authorities and others are private). Talk about how it can be someone's job to

provide other people's leisure activities and that this means that the worker has to be paid, directly or indirectly, by the people doing this activity.

Do people who work in the leisure industries like to take their relaxation in the same way? Or would they rather do something completely different in their spare time? Did they start in this work because it gave them more opportunities for an activity they enjoyed? How does it feel to be working doing something that other people do just for fun?

### Further activities
Ask the children to draw pictures of people who do work that other people do for fun (professional football, gardening). Find out how local services are provided. What proportion of the local authority's budget goes on leisure activities?

## 9. The library

### Foundation subject links
English.

### Age range
Seven to eleven.

### Group size
Six to eight and the whole class.

### What you need
Paper, pencils.

### What to do
Visit the local library to talk with the staff (choose a time that is unlikely to be busy). Ask a local councillor on the library committee to come to talk with the class at a later

date. Ask the children to examine the local community's need for a library. They might carry out a survey of how much the public make use of public libraries. How many people visit the library and how often? How many never visit a library?

Ask the library staff about the services that they provide and who makes use of them. Find out how much it costs to provide library services. How much money is spent on staff, buildings and books?

Talk with a local councillor about why the council provides library services. Ask the councillor how they decide on how much to spend on these activities.

# 10. Links with Europe

### Foundation subject links
Geography, English.

### Age range
Seven to eleven.

### Group size
Six to eight.

### What you need
Maps of Europe and the world.

### What to do
Ask the children to find out what local links there are with Europe and other countries. They could investigate: the origins of food in the shops, television programmes that feature other countries, sporting links and holidays.

Ask the children to find out which of these countries are members of the European Community, which are from Europe but outside the Community and which are outside Europe. They could also look at links with countries of the Commonwealth.

Different groups of children could present their findings in different ways, perhaps through a play, a meal or a map.

### Further activity
Ask the class to find out about other groups of countries (the Commonwealth, the CIS, the non-aligned movement and the 'Third world').

# 11. Our local schools

### Foundation subject links
English, geography.

### Age range
Five to eleven.

### Group size
Six to eight.

### What you need
A large-scale local map; contacts with local schools; felt-tipped pens.

### What to do
Ask the groups to study a local map and locate all the schools that they know. They might mark different types of school (primary, nursery, secondary) in different ways. Ask them to think of what they know about these schools. What links does your school have with them? For example, shared facilities (libraries, swimming pools) or sports matches that are played. Do the schools 'catchment areas' overlap?

Invite some children from other schools to visit your school to describe the differences. Alternatively, arrange for some of the children in the class to visit other local schools.

# 12. Which languages can you speak?

## Foundation subject links
English, geography, history, mathematics.

## Age range
Seven to eleven.

## Group size
The whole class and small groups.

## What you need
Paper, clipboards, pencils, photocopiable page 191; materials for making a poster.

## What to do
There are probably several hundred different first or community languages spoken by children in our schools.

Some primary schools have 30 to 40 different languages represented. Bilingualism is a valuable skill and an important asset.

Ask the children to find out how many languages are spoken in the school. How many children speak two, three or more languages? How many of them can read or write in languages other than English? Do their parents speak languages that they cannot speak?

Help the children to draw up a questionnaire to use in the school, (photocopiable page 191 may be of use). Make sufficient copies so that every child in the school can be interviewed. Arrange for groups of children from your class to visit other classes to complete their questionnaires. You may need to ensure that bilingual children from your class visit particular classes, so that they can explain to children what is going on.

Encourage the children to make tally charts, bar graphs and pie charts to show the range of languages being spoken. They could use the school computer and a data-handling package to sort out the collected data.

Does the proportion of children speaking different languages change with older classes? Are there any particular combinations of languages that are often found together (for example Urdu/Arabic, Bengali/Arabic), and if so, can the children find out why? Can they locate the origins of the various language groups on the world map?

Ask the children to make lists of children who are fluent bilingual speakers and the languages that they speak. Give these to all class teachers and helpers, so that they know which children to call on for help when another child is beginning to speak English.

## Further activity
The children could make a poster to welcome visitors to the school. Get the word 'Welcome' written in as many different languages as possible (certainly all those spoken by the children in the school).

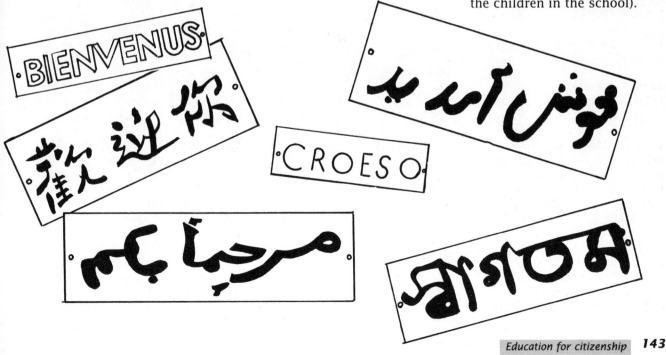

# 13. First societies

## Foundation subject links
History, English.

## Age range
Seven to eleven.

## Group size
The whole class, divided into groups of about six.

## What you need
Class materials on early societies studied in history.

## What to do
As part of a history project on an early civilisation (perhaps ancient Egypt, Greece, the Roman Empire or the Indus Valley), ask the children to look at the different laws and customs that developed. How do these laws and customs differ from the ones that apply today?

Ask groups of children to role-play conflicts within early societies and the ways in which these might have been resolved. This is a useful way of developing empathy with other times and could become a basis for making comparisons and contrasts with the present.

## Further activity
Ask the children to create laws, rules and customs for an imaginary early society. Can the children explain why they are made? Ask them to act them out in role-play to see if they work.

# 14. A class council

## Foundation subject links
English.

## Age range
Five to eleven.

## Group size
The whole class.

## What you need
Paper, pens, pencils, materials for making posters.

## What to do
Organise a class council. Discuss matters of concern to the children, for example, rules for behaviour in the classroom during wet play, or possible destinations for the end-of-term outing or class assemblies.

How many people will be needed on the council? How will they be chosen? Many children will suggest ideas they have heard about from adults and the media (elections, election campaigns, voting). You will need to help them organise elections (opportunities for posters and campaign talks, working out how the vote can be secret and so on).

How will the council operate? Will representatives collect views from the rest of the class? How will they report back to the class on what has been discussed?

## Further activity
If the activity is successful, call for a fresh election at the beginning of the next term. Will the same children stand again for election? Will they be successful?

# 15. Changes, changes

## Foundation subject links
History, English, geography.

## Age range
Five to eleven.

## Group size
Six to eight.

## What you need
Elderly people prepared to talk with the children about life when they were young.

## What to do
Ask each group of children to talk with an elderly person about families in the past. Discuss what questions might be asked beforehand, for example, about different jobs or roles within the family, about changes within families as members leave or move and about other relations who may have lived near by.

When the groups have finished their interviews, they could compare their findings. They might each present short role-plays or scenes of family life in the past, and draw comparisons and contrasts both between the families represented, and with their own families today.

# 16. An ideal society

## Foundation subject links
English.

## Age range
Seven to eleven.

## Group size
Three to four, then the whole class.

## What you need
Paper, pens.

## What to do
Arrange the children in friendship groups of three to four children. Each group is to plan independently an ideal society. Ask the children questions to help them. How will it be organised? What sort of rules will it have? How will these rules be made? How will the society be governed or run? What sort of money will it have? How will the money be divided?

The children could write a description of the society and its rules or draw a picture. Encourage the children to consider how the society will work, rather than spend the time making futuristic drawings!

Ask each group to make a presentation to the rest of the class about their ideal society. Encourage the children to answer questions and criticisms from the other children. After all the groups have made their presentations, the children could vote on the best society.

## Further activity
Read the class stories about other 'ideal societies', such as *The Lord of the Flies* by William Golding (Faber) or *Animal Farm* by George Orwell (Penguin). Discuss with the children what these societies were trying to achieve and how and why things did not work out as expected.

## 17. Anti-social behaviour

### Foundation subject links
English, mathematics, geography.

### Age range
Nine to eleven.

### Group size
The whole class, divided into groups of six to eight on occasions.

### What you need
Maps of the local area, clipboards, paper, pens.

### What to do
As part of a study of the local environment, discuss with the children any antisocial activity they may have seen in the area. This might be throwing litter in the street, inconsiderate or dangerous parking, graffiti or playing dangerously near traffic (the activities will vary from area to area).

Ask the children how they can find out the extent of the problem. Can they measure how much of a problem it is? Where does it happen? When does it happen? Who do they think is responsible?

Help the children to organise a survey of the area. They could arrange to interview local people to find out their views and make maps of where the problem seems to be the worst.

Discuss with the class ways in which they think the problem might be solved. Different groups could try working on different solutions. Ask each group to present their ideas to the rest of the class.

### Further activity
Invite an appropriate authority to school to discuss the ideas with the class, for example, a local environmental health officer or a local police officer (it will depend on the particular problem).

## 18. A century of service?

### Foundation subject links
English, history.

### Age range
Seven to eleven.

### Group size
The whole class and groups of six to eight.

### What you need
Reference materials about public services, particularly archive material about these in the local area (the public library should be able to help); contact with local people who are involved in providing one of these services.

## Fire Brigade

### What to do

Identify one or two local services that the children are interested in (possibilities include libraries, the police station, fire brigade, refuse collection or even schools). Ask the children to investigate the current provision of this service, focusing on who needs the service and how it is provided and paid for.

Ask the groups of children to examine how this service was provided in the past. Local archive material may help with specific local data, supplemented by appropriate history reference books that may provide more general information and context.

Ask the class to construct a time-line that shows how the changes have taken place in the provision of this service. Can the children identify the differences in provision? Why? Can they tell when the changes occurred?

### Further activity

Invite people who provide the service today to visit the class and look at the work that has been done. Ask them to tell the children what they do in their work.

## 19. The health centre

### Foundation subject links

English, geography, science.

### Age range

Seven to eleven.

### Group size

The whole class, divided into groups of six to eight where appropriate.

### What you need

Access to a local health centre, so that the children can talk to the different people who work there; pencils, paper, coloured pencils or felt-tipped pens.

### What to do

Arrange for the class to study the local health centre as a workplace. They could investigate the range of people who work there, how they are organised and administered, and the problems that they have in meeting the public's needs.

Groups might consider specific aspects of the centre's activities. For example, one group might ask how the centre is paid for, how much it costs to run and how the money is spent. Another group might concentrate on the views of users about the level of provision and whether it meets their needs.

Encourage the children to make a class exhibition or presentation on the work of the health centre and its relationship with the local community. Invite members of the centre to comment on the work of the class.

### Further activity

A class assembly or a class book could consolidate much of the work and make it accessible to other children in the school.

# 20. Journeys around the world

## Foundation subject links
Geography, English, history, mathematics.

## Age range
Seven to eleven.

## Group size
Six to eight.

## What you need
World maps, travel brochures, coloured string or wool, map pins.

## What to do
Ask the class to compile lists of all the journeys that they and their families have made around the world. Locate the various journeys on local, national and world maps. Create a large world map that shows the journeys of families, for example, from Britain on holiday and perhaps to the UK as immigrants. Use coloured string or wool to show the journeys and add pictures of the places involved from travel brochures.

Find out about areas that several people have moved from to the locality. What cultural and social customs have they brought with them? How have they adapted and changed in this country? Invite parents and other members of the community to talk with the class about why people moved to Britain and what changes they have seen.

# 21. The school that I'd like

## Foundation subject links
English, geography and history.

## Age range
Seven to eleven.

## Group size
Three to four.

## What you need
Photocopiable page 192, pencils.

## What to do
Ask each group to work independently of the others. Their task is to plan an ideal school. What would it do? What would it look like? While different groups will interpret this in different ways, try to ensure that they all consider more than the physical appearance and layout (though this is not unimportant). They may need to consider a number of issues:
• What is the school for?
• Who will come to the school? (ages, how many)
• What sort of person is needed to teach at the school?
• What things will the school need – books, equipment, teachers, other adults, spaces and rooms, other facilities – toilets, lunches and so on.

Photocopiable page 192 may help the groups organise their thoughts at this stage – but it is only intended as a prompt and is not intended to be used as a finished presentation.

When the children have thought about and discussed these sorts of questions, they might begin to plan the physical appearance of the school and how it would operate. Encourage the children to make necessary measurements and evaluations of their existing premises and resources, and to ask questions of adults in the school about their roles and duties.

Each group should aim to make a short presentation to the rest of the class to explain their ideas. When several groups have put forward their ideas, encourage the class to ask questions and to compare plans.

## Further activity
Discuss with the class what their proposals might cost and how they might be implemented. Ask the chair of the school governing body to listen to the children's plans and to discuss them.

# CHAPTER 6

# Project themes

It was suggested in the Introduction that various parts of the cross-curricular themes might be included either within the teaching of a particular subject, or as part of an integrated topic or theme.

There is a third way in which cross-curricular themes might sometimes be approached in the primary school: by using the theme itself as a unifying focus for a project or topic. Through such a project, various aspects of the foundation subjects will be addressed; in addition, the work will be securely located within a holistic approach to the curriculum.

The following pages outline eight suggestions for such projects. Each double-page chart lays out ideas for a project that may last up to half a term. The 'Curriculum facts' section indicates the main focus of the project, suggests an age range and identifies the foundation subjects that are most clearly present. 'Planning' indicates some of the preparatory work which might be necessary before beginning, while 'Starting point' gives some opening activities.

The ideas that follow might be tackled in parallel by different groups in the class, or undertaken by all the children. The order of these activities need not necessarily be as indicated. The 'Finishing point' suggests a useful way of wrapping up the project with your class, and of bringing all the various elements and activities together.

# People around us

## Curriculum facts

An economic and industrial understanding project for
five- to seven-year-olds.
**Related curriculum areas:** English, geography, history,
mathematics.

This project focuses on the economic interrelationships of
people who work in the vicinity of the school. Focusing on the
familiar context of the locality, children meet people and talk
about their working lives.

## Planning

Before you start with the class, list all the various people who
work in the immediate locality around the school, of whom
the children might be aware. This may include parents, local
shop workers, people working on the street (police officers,
street cleaners, etc.), and people calling at the school. Make
arrangements for some of them to come to the class to talk to
groups of children about their work.

Collect magazine and newspaper photographs showing
people doing everyday tasks. Many of those from
advertisements may reflect stereotypical views of work, and
you may wish to draw attention to this and to seek out
contrasting examples.

## Starting point

Talk with the children
about all the people whom
they have seen working in
and around the school.
Make a list for the class
to see.

Ask the children to paint
or draw different workers,
sharing out different
people from the list. Mount
these as a collage.

Talk about the different
kinds of jobs that the
children think these
workers have to do.

## Interviewing

Invite a local worker into
the class to talk with a
small group about their
work. Where else do they
work? Who do they work
with? Do they enjoy it?
Which parts of their job do
they not like?

Children can paint and
draw their subject at work
and make an illustrated
book about the person's
working day, showing the
sequence of different
activities.

This activity could be
repeated with other
workers and with other
groups of children.

## Sets and sorting

Make a set of card figures,
each representing a
different local worker.
(These could be made by
the children.) Ask a group
to sort the figures into sets
drawn on large sheets of
paper, using various
criteria – perhaps into male
jobs/female jobs/either
male or female; or
outdoor/indoor; or 'people
I know'/'people I don't
know'. Discuss if there are
any problems in putting
particular pictures in sets.

### Role-play

Collect hats or pieces of costume associated with particular local workers. Children can dress up in these and take on roles, drawing from their observations and talks with people at work. You could introduce incidents where two or more workers meet: a police officer, a cleaner and a postal worker. What do they say to each other?

### A street survey

Take a small group to watch people passing by on the street. Who is at work and who is not? How can they tell? Take pictures of workers or ask the children to draw them. How many different workers did they see in their survey? Will a different group, going at a different time of day, meet other workers? Mount a display to show the results of the survey.

### Weather check

Discuss with the children how the weather may affect different people who work in the local area. Make a list of different local jobs – street cleaner, ice-cream seller, a crossing patrol person and so on, and then ask the children to imagine each person at work on a hot day, a cold day, a wet day... Does the job change? Do the workers do different things, wear different clothes?

### Popular jobs

Discuss which work the children think that they would most like to do themselves. Ask them to think about what they have found out from the people they have spoken to.

### Working times

Ask the children to find out at what times different local people are working. Depending on the age of the children, this may be related to actual times or to periods of the day (morning, evening, night, etc.). Children could ask people about their hours of work. The class or group could make a frieze showing a period of 24 hours and stick pictures of individual workers at the appropriate times. Alternatively, they could make circles representing 24 hours for each person and shade in the hours that they work.

### Changes at work

Ask the children to interview an older worker about how their job, and the local area, have changed over their working life. What was it like when they first started work? What differences can they see now? Children could make a series of pictures in a frieze, showing the changes over time. They could ask other people about their ideas about changes and see if they are the same.

### Coming into school

Ask the children to keep a record of all the different people who come to work at the school. Many will be regular people – teachers, cleaners, cooks; many will come less often – nurses, delivery people, inspectors. What do they all do? Ask the children to interview them and find out.

### Interconnections

Make a class display of all the people who work in the area around the school. Link together the pictures of people who sometimes work together, or who need to rely on other workers to do their jobs properly. Discuss how people depend on each other.

### Finishing point

Organise a class assembly that shows off all the different facets of the work that has been done; or ask the children to organise and hold a class tea party, inviting in as many local people and parents as possible to see the results of the project.

# Investigating a workplace

## Curriculum facts

An economic and industrial understanding project for seven- to eleven-year-olds.
**Related curriculum areas:** English, mathematics, geography, technology.

This project focuses on a detailed study of a local office, factory, shop or other workplace such as a hospital or a park. The emphasis is on meeting and talking to as many as possible of the people who work together in the same organisation.

## Planning

Before you start work with the class, find a local workplace that will cooperate with the school. Parents and governors may be able to suggest suitable locations. It is worth allowing some time for planning visits to meet various people who work there.

Make a preliminary visit to see the activities and to decide which curricular links are particularly appropriate. Discuss how the children can best see the processes involved, bearing in mind both providing a coherent learning experience and safety. Try to plan for a good cross-section of people – shop-floor workers, supervisors, office staff and trade unionists, as well as managers.

## Starting point

A visit to the workplace is an important early experience, but it can help to have a short discussion with the children immediately beforehand. What do they expect to see? What do they already know about what happens there? Even if their expectations are not very realistic, the fact that they have made them explicit will allow them to make some sharp contrasts on the visit.

## Interviews

Arrange as many interviews as possible between different groups of children and workers. It is often better to have a range of areas to be discussed, rather than a precise list of questions to ask. Making a tape-recording is usually a better form of record than trying to make notes during the talk.

## The first visit

Expect the first visit to concentrate on the basics of what happens at the workplace. Try to follow through the line of production or the provision of a particular service, so that the children see a logical progression. Take photographs and keep notes yourself, as well as encouraging children to sketch and make notes. Photographs and names of the individuals the children talk to will be invaluable in later class discusions and displays.

## Production flow

Ask the class to cooperate in making charts or pictures that show how the various parts, sections or departments of the organisation work together. In a factory, this may involve the flow of production, from stores through to packaging: in a service industry, it may be more useful to follow a client's passage through the organisation.

## Who does what

Discuss with the children why work is often broken down into different stages, with specialisation taking place. If this happens, workers at each stage are dependent on other groups doing their part of the work efficiently. Organise a simulation of a production line in class and experiment with how the different groups need to work together to get the work done.

## Materials in use

Collect samples of the materials that are used in production. Encourage the children to discuss their qualities. Why do they think that these particular materials have been chosen? Perhaps they could carry out tests on them. Afterwards they could discuss their findings with the people at the workplace.

## Waste products

Look at the materials that are not used by the firm and are disposed of as rubbish, waste or effluent. What steps does the workplace use to ensure safe disposal, recycling or minimisation of waste? Can the children safely explore alternative uses of by-products?

## Who's in charge?

Discuss the way in which the workplace is organised. Most workplaces have a hierarchical organisation. Encourage the children to work out what this might be by asking individuals who tells them what to do, and to whom they can give instructions. Draw hierarchy charts or make a mobile that explains the structure. Discuss how these compare with the school and other organisations.

## The second visit

Repeated visits to a workplace encourage different kinds of questions: once an understanding of the practical arrangements has been grasped, children ask more detailed questions about organisation and working relations. Ideas and suppositions discussed in class after the impressions of the first visit can be tested against a second chance to talk with the workers. It is also useful to invite them to school, to continue the discussion there and to show them the work done by the children.

## Wages

In many organisations it is possible to find out the ranges of pay for particular categories of work, though not, of course, any individual's pay. Collect together these details and discuss the existing pay differentials. Do the differences in skills, responsibility, training and status justify the existing range? Make models of different workers and put them on plinths whose heights represent their wages.

## Safety first

Is the workplace safe? Ask the children to look for all the possible danger points around the workplace. What efforts are made to prevent accidents and keep people safe? Encourage the children to devise safety posters to warn people of potential dangers. Discuss safety conditions with trade union representatives.

## Finishing point

Organise a classroom display of all the work that was done during the project and send invitations to the workplace for representatives to visit the school and see the work.

# Ourselves

## Curriculum facts

A health education project for five- to seven-year-olds.
**Related curriculum areas:** science, English, physical education.

This project looks at children's lives – their bodies, their social group and how they live. It combines aspects of health education with a range of local social and environmental issues.

## Planning

A number of human and other resources will need to be assembled before the project can take off. Children's parents will need to be approached so that they are ready for the investigation. It will help to involve some parents of much younger children and also to approach one or two elderly people who are willing to talk about ageing.

## Starting point

A good beginning is to ask the children to define themselves in a series of activities: painting self-portraits, describing their families, listing their favourite meals, drinks and games. One activity might be the compilation of a class database on the computer, using a program such as OURFACTS.

## Eating

Discuss favourite foods. What do children think different foods do to their bodies? Many children think that particular foods go to make particular parts of their body grow. Discuss different types of nutrients: proteins, carbohydrates, fats and vitamins. Which foods are rich in each of these?

## Washing

Ask the class why we wash ourselves. What would happen if we did not? A wide variety of answers usually materialise. Ask the children to experiment with finding the most effective soap or cleansing agent to remove dirt (e.g., paint) from hands.

## Babies

What were we like as babies? Ask the children to bring in their baby photographs. See if they can tell who was who. Ask other teachers to bring in their baby photographs and show them to the children. How have they changed?

Invite in a parent with a young baby and let the class watch it being cared for, fed, changed, etc. What things do babies need done for them that children at school can do for themselves? What things do the children still need help with?

## Running, jumping...

What does exercise do to the body? Ask the children why they think exercise is important and what happens to their bodies when they exercise. Then ask them to try it out, looking at how their hearts beat faster, their breathing rate changes, their skin sweats and their muscles tire. **NB** All children doing this activity must be physically fit. No child who is excused games or PE activities on medical grounds should be allowed to be the subject of this activity.

## Standing still, sleeping

Discuss what happens when your body rests. Experiment with the children lying still and looking at the same factors as they did when they exercised. Talk about why people need to sleep and what happens if they miss their sleep. Ask the children to draw and paint themselves walking, running, resting and sleeping.

## Caring for people

Talk about how everyone relies on other people to do some things for them. What sort of things do the children need other people to do for them? What can they do to help other people? Draw and label pictures of people who help us and people we help. Can the children imagine themselves getting older? Ask them to draw themselves as they might look then.

## The health centre

Visit a local health centre with a group of children or try to arrange for some of its employees to visit the school. Ask the children to find out what different tasks are done by the centre and how it helps local people keep healthy and well. Use simple props to encourage role-play based on the health centre in the home corner.

## Families

People who live together tend to care for each other in a variety of ways. Who do we live with? What different kinds of family are there represented in our class? Ask the children to create pictures and collages to show nuclear and extended families, and talk about the different ways in which family members care for each other.

## Friends

What friendship groups do the children belong to? What sets of friends are there – on the same street, in the playground, in groups and communities outside the school? What do the various groups of friends do together and how do these activities differ? Create a class collage of children's games.

## Getting older

Encourage the children to think about what will happen as they become older. What different sorts of care might elderly people need? There may be elderly people willing to come into school or a day centre near the school that groups of children could visit, where they can talk to older people about the effects of ageing and the needs of the elderly.

## Finishing point

Make a class display on the themes of 'Our bodies' and 'Change'. There could be sections showing how people stay healthy and well at different stages of their life. Invite parents and other classes to see the display. Groups of children could act as guides to explain the work to visitors.

# What can I do?

## Curriculum facts

A careers education and guidance project for seven- to eleven-year-olds.
**Related curriculum area:** English.

This project encourages children to develop a sense of identity and to relate this to knowledge of their own development and of working life, while encouraging them to explore their aspirations.

## Planning

This project will not involve large amounts of planning time before the work in class begins. But, as it progresses, and the children's individual ideas and programmes develop, you will need to organise and collect material about specific occupations.

## Team building

Building on the previous activity, ask the children to arrange themselves into groups that have a wide range of talents. They must build groups that can do as wide a range of things as possible. You might want to limit the group size to, say, five or six. Ask the groups to tackle tasks collaboratively (in any appropriate curricular activity), and to think about how all members of the team make their own particular contribution.

## Starting point

Ask the children to think about what they would like to do for a living when they grow up. They could draw themselves at work and write what they know about the particular occupation that they have chosen. Some will fantasise and others will make unrealistic choices: but at this stage, allow anything. As the processes are completed, encourage the children to exchange ideas and explain their choices to each other.

## Talent listing

Tell the class that everyone can do some things better than others. Ask the children to list the things that they are good at: encourage them to think about a wide range of skills and activities, not simply 'academic' ones – some might be good at caring for people, or keeping things tidy or cheering other people up. (They might also list the things that they like doing and see if the two lists overlap!)

## We can...

Ask each team to imagine that they are a group looking for tasks. They need to get someone to commission them to do something – something that they would be good at as a team, using all their talents, and something that they would enjoy doing. Each team must write a leaflet, setting out the abilities of the group. (Some members of the group will be better at this activity than others: how can they work so that everyone can contribute?)

## What's my line?

Individual children should select different jobs and find out what they entail. In turn, each child should mime some activity connected with the work and then answer questions from the rest of the class/ group, who try to find out what job has been chosen.

## Job ideas

Ask the children to think about a range of jobs that they might be suited for: they should make individual lists, but should be allowed to work together in teams (thus making suggestions to each other and discussing the appropriateness of particular ideas). Their lists and ideas will be more varied and more linked to their likes and aptitudes, than those made in the starting activity in this project.

## A working day

Ask the children to imagine themselves at work in one of the occupations that they have chosen. What will their day be like? Ask them to draw a strip cartoon of the working (and non-working) day – an hour-by-hour picture.

## Looking into the future

The children should listen to each other's ideas and then imagine the whole class in twenty years' time. What will they all be doing? Ask them to write a story or paint a picture of some of their friends in the future, at work or at leisure.

## And a time to rest?

What would the children like to do in their spare time when they are adult? If they have chosen occupations that they like doing, will they continue with them after work – does the council gardener dig his own garden at the weekend? Do professional footballers play football with their friends on their day off?

## Research into training

Encourage individual children to find out more about some of the occupations they have chosen. Ask if their idea of what a working day might look like matches what they find out. Ask them to find out what particular skills or talents are necessary for the job. What sort of training or preparation is needed? When is this done, and where? Each child could build up a small information book.

## Moving up

Discuss as a class what the children will be doing in the school when they are older or what they will be doing at secondary school. What sort of skills will they have developed in two or three years' time? What would they like to develop? Can they set themselves targets that might help them to achieve them?

## Finishing point

Present a class assembly to the school based on what the class think they will be doing in the future – next year, in three years, five years, ten years and twenty years. This might take the form of a series of playlets written by the children or of a mime to a narrative read by one of the children.

# Creating a garden

## Curriculum facts

An environmental education project for five- to seven-year-olds.
**Related curriculum areas:** science, geography, English, technology.

This project centres on the practical activity of designing and making a small garden for the school, in which children consider environmental issues in context, drawing on intellectual, emotional and social skills.

## Planning

While this project could be run purely as a planning activity, it would be much more effective if a school garden area could be developed. If this is feasible, this will require some preparation: finding resources, arranging help from parents and arranging times when work can be done. In all of this, as much planning activity as possible should be left to the children: this will mean that your preparation will have to allow for a range of possible outcomes, depending on their decisions!

## Starting point

Take the children to look at the area that is to be developed as a garden. Help them measure it, photograph it and note down what it is like at present. Perhaps an equivalent area could be marked out in the classroom or a large plan made of the area.

## Making plans

Using a large plan of the area or a marked-out equivalent area, discuss and make alternative plans of how the garden might be developed. Perhaps several alternatives might be drawn, both as plans and as pictures. Ask the children to compare and contrast the different ideas. Which ones will help preserve the environment or do the least damage to it?

## What do we want?

Brainstorm with the class to find out all the possible things that could be done with the area. What would different people like? What sort of garden: a wildlife garden, or lots of bright flowers to attract minibeasts and butterflies? Talk about why one area cannot do everything. Whose ideas are important in this? How can they be found out? What precautions must the children take to not pollute the area and to make it safe for children and animals?

## How much will it cost? How long will it take?

Ask the class to think about the practicalities of their ideas. What materials are needed for each idea? In what quantities? What will they cost? When lists of materials have been made, take a group of children to a garden centre or a builder's merchant to find out how much items cost. Then ask them to work out how much time they think each idea will involve. Ask them to think about all the environmental costs each project will involve.

## Keeping a record

Ask the children to discuss the alternative schemes and to come to a decision about which one to pursue. Having made a choice, more detailed plans and timescales could be worked out. Who will do the work? When? Exactly how much of each material will be needed? When will it be needed? How much will it cost? How will it be paid for? Encourage a group of children to keep records of what happens and when.

## Getting ready

Help the children break down the necessary tasks into manageable units, so that they can see how they will develop and be accomplished.

## Places to watch

Where are good places to stand to see the plant and animal life in the garden? Where is the least damage done? Can particular places for viewing be created – perhaps with proper places to stand? Are there special places to see certain things?

## Planting

When planting – seeds, cuttings, seedlings – ask the children to watch carefully how the new plants establish themselves. What do they need for healthy growth: water, protection from frost and damage, and so on. How can the children ensure that the plants will continue to get these in the new garden?

## Digging

As each stage is completed, ask the children to think how what they are doing is affecting the environment. When they are digging, for example, they could look at the minibeasts and worms that are disturbed. What do they need for a healthy life? What do they contribute to the soil?

## Tending

As the garden develops, point out to the children how plants and minibeasts compete for space and food. Some plants tend to dominate others. If they want a variety of plants, they may have to cut back some of the more dominant plants to let others develop.

## Notices

When the garden is established and the children are familiar with what is to be seen, ask them to think about other users. What would they like to see? Would notices or signs be useful – perhaps telling the visitors where to stand or what to look for? Can the children design and make these signs?

## Finishing point

Celebrate the establishment of the garden with a garden party – as long as it does not cause environmental damage! Ask the children to make a Garden Book, with photographs and paintings of the garden around the year. They could set up a camera in a regular spot and take a photograph on the same day each month.

# Conserve, recycle, purify and survive

## Curriculum facts

An environmental education project for seven- to eleven-year-olds.
**Related curriculum areas:** science, technology, geography, English, mathematics.

A project which develops children's concerns about environmental dangers, looking at contemporary problems of waste disposal, shortages of raw materials and pollution in the local environment.

## Planning

Make your own survey of the local area, looking for particular locations where there are the best opportunities for looking at domestic or commercial waste and pollution. This might be the local council's refuse department or recycling unit, or a local firm that has to dispose of waste materials. Ideally, it should be a site close enough to the school to be visited frequently.

Make contact with the people responsible and explain that you would like your children to investigate the problem and how the council/group/company have tackled it. It will be very useful to get cooperation from the earliest stages. Get advice from them on any safety aspects: while many waste products will be safe for children to handle, others may need to be observed with caution. Ensure that all the class know your safety rules and why they have been made, and that they follow them.

## Starting point

Begin with a short class discussion on the problems of pollution and waste disposal. The children will probably already have views on the subject, though they may see it in very simple terms of blame and fault, and see remedies as being simple and easy to implement. Turn the discussion to the local issue that they are to investigate: what do they know about it already? Explain that their enquiry will begin by establishing the scale of the problem.

## How much?

Visit the site and look at the problem. Is it the disposal of rubbish and scrap, the cleaning of waste products before they can be released, using and wasting fewer materials or a combination of these? How much material/scrap is involved in a day? Can the children calculate the size of the problem over a year? What volumes are involved? Measure out areas in the playground or calculate 'classroomfuls' to help the class appreciate the scale of the problem.

## When?

Continue the investigation into the scale of the problem by finding out whether the problem is constant or whether it varies in scale over the day, from day to day or over the year. Can the children measure what is happening over time? Can they ask questions of people at the work site or find out why there are changes over time? They could also investigate if the problem is worse than it used to be or whether matters have improved and why.

## Where?

Another variable that the children might investigate is the location of the problem: are there particular points in the site that are worse than others? Why should this be?

## Ideas for re-using

Are there any ways in which scrap material could be used? If it is possible and safe, ask if the children can take samples of scrap to experiment with. Investigate the qualities of the materials and try finding alternative uses through making toys, simple domestic items and so on.

## Appearances

Human activity can change the appearance of the environment, as well as its physical characteristics. Ask the children to redesign the business so that it blends in better and stands out less. What landscaping or building design would help this? (This activity may not be suitable for all sites, particularly if the 'natural' environment is no longer discernible.)

## In the longer term

Ask the class or a group to look at what might happen in the future if local consumption of resources and pollution continues unchecked and what might be possible with greater planning and control. They could prepare alternative scenarios showing possible outcomes.

## Finding out why

No one deliberately sets out to cause pollution or to waste resources. (It may be important to help make this clear to the class during the project.) So why is there a problem? Encourage the children to talk with the people responsible about the following issues:

• the historic dimension – some of the dangers and problems that we are now concerned with were not adequately known about in the past;

• the problem of scale – small-scale pollution was often contained or dealt with by the local balance of nature;

• economic dimensions – it costs to clean up the environment and manufacturers have to pass most of those costs on to consumers. If rival manufacturers do not spend the same on pollution control, then their products are cheaper and are bought by the public instead of the more expensive, non-polluting goods.

## Ideas for cleaning up

Back in school, ask the children for other suggestions for cleaning up the waste products. Are there other ways of making sure that fewer dangerous effluents reach the rivers and air? Can they be tested or tried out in some way?

## Counting the cost

This could be extended into considering the costs of either course of action. Children could draw up a detailed profit-and-loss account of all the advantages of each course of action – and the costs that each would bring.

## What's being done?

Nearly all businesses are now aware of the problems of pollution and waste, and are anxious to tackle them – both because of legislation and the pressure of public opinion. Ask the children to find out what the business is doing now and what changes it is making.

## Finishing point

Ask the children to create a class book of ideas about the problem and its possible solutions, and present it to the local business. They could also make an assembly production based on the investigation. Invite local environmental health officers and members of the company to see it.

# Running our classroom

## Curriculum facts

An education for citizenship project for five- to seven-year-olds.
**Related curriculum areas:** English, technology.

A project which allows children to explore the social problems of organising their own class, of being aware of the needs of other people, and drawing up social rules and systems that allow the class to run smoothly.

## Planning

This project calls for the class teacher to allow the children to discuss and experiment with classroom routines, trying to find out ways in which they might organise them better. It helps if the class are already settled into a well-established and straightforward pattern of working and are then encouraged to experiment with one aspect of the pattern at a time. Often, they may conclude that your system was best: occasionally, they will devise a system that is better! It is important to try, wherever possible, to allow them the freedom to discuss and try ideas out and not simply to justify your existing way of working.

## Getting in and out

Talk about how children enter and leave (and move about) the classroom. Are there any difficulties? What do they like and dislike? What problems do they cause other people? Can they think of different ways of tackling the difficulties? There may be several suggestions: try out each for half a day and at the end of the trials discuss which they thought worked best. Could it be made any better?

## Starting point

Ask the children to see if they can make a list of all the rules they have to follow in the classroom. You could write these down with them if this helps. Encourage them to discuss the rules together. Ask if these are all rules that they have been told or if they are simply ones that they have seen at work. What do they think are the reasons for each?

## The class day

Explain that the children are going to look at the way that the class is run and see if they can find ways to make it better. What are all the various activities that have to be fitted into the school day? Make a class book or display showing each activity – curricular activities, times for eating, play and physical activities, and so on. Use this book/display as a reference item in the rest of the project to remind the children of the things that they have to allow to happen.

## Where shall we work?

Draw up a large plan of the classroom, showing individual and group areas. Discuss this with groups of children, helping them identify locations and understand how the plan works. Discuss with the children how the class might be re-organised, so that different things happened in different places. Can they suggest alternatives? What sorts of spaces do they need for different activities such as painting, quiet reading, home corners, sand trays, water activities, writing? Can the plan be improved?

## How do we like working?

Talk with the whole class about what makes it easy to enjoy working at school. Then ask groups to think if they can work out ideas for rules or ways of working that would help make it easier to work well. Bring all the ideas together and see if the class can improve on them. Then try out some of them, perhaps one at a time or several ideas together. After a trial, talk about whether things have improved.

## What do we need?

In a class discussion, ask the children to look around and identify all the things that they sometimes need to go to to use, or to bring to their own working space. Are these things easy to get? Are they convenient? Are there any particular hazards? Could there be a better arrangement? Try out some alternatives.

## Areas we share: the home corner

Focus on one classroom area at a time: what makes the home corner work well? What sorts of rules or systems of working might help it work better? A maximum number of people at a time? A timetable for its use? Having other particular activities away from it? Rules about tidying up?

## Individuals and groups

Talk about the different ways in which the class works: how sometimes children work on their own and sometimes together. What does each way of working need in terms of space, surrounding noise, access to materials and so on? How often do they switch from individual to group work and vice versa in a day?

## Times for working

Discuss if it is possible or sensible to do some of the various classroom activities in a different order. What times do the children know that they cannot change and why? (They may need some encouragement to recognise that other people use the hall when they are not there or that the dinner staff need to have fixed times.) Within such flexibility as you do have, try out one or two re-schedulings and discuss the consequences.

## Areas we share: books and reading spaces

Talk about the area where books are kept and stories read, either individually or to the class as a whole. What sort of areas does reading need? How do books need to be cared for? Are there ways of making these conditions easier or more possible?

## Areas we share: storage spaces

Talk about the places where things are kept about the room: paints, aprons, water, sand, construction materials, paper. How do they need to be treated or cared for to make the classroom work well for everyone? Are there particular rules that would make it easier?

## Finishing point

Having worked their way around the classroom, discuss with the class all the changes that they have suggested and tried out. Talk about how some worked, while others were less successful. Make up a class improvement book. Talk about how rules are made, whether they work or not and how they can be changed and improved.

# Island society

## Curriculum facts

An education for citizenship project for seven- to eleven-year-olds.
**Related curriculum areas:** English, geography, technology.

A project which allows children to explore through role-play how they might form their own small society, devising and using rules that govern it, and finding ways to accept and tolerate differences in views.

## Planning

This extended role-play needs a series of times when groups of children can discuss problems together. It will be helpful for discussion and comparison if different groups could undertake similar activities at the same time. Generally, this does not involve large spaces. Modelling, mapping and other writing work may be associated with the role-play if you wish. After each suggested activity, it will be helpful to bring the class together to hear how different groups responded, to allow you to draw out similarities and differences, and to allow the class to see parallels with 'real-life' situations.

## Jobs to be done

Ask the groups to think about all the different tasks that will need to be tackled if they are to survive on the island. Some of these will be daily tasks, others will be less frequent. Some will take a lot of time, some will be boring, others will be exciting. Can the children list the jobs? Can they find a fair way to get them all done?

## Starting point

Establish a school voyage through role-play. Set the class off on a cruise: establish a routine of different cabins (to set up groups), daily activities, postcards home. Then announce a shipwreck: different groups are dispersed to different desert islands.

## Priorities

On the island, the first task for each group is to find out what is on their island and to decide what they must tackle first. They could draw maps of their islands, agreeing on what resources there are and what dangers they face. They need to think about food, safety, shelter and perhaps rescue. How do they decide?

## Squabbles

Not everyone will like the jobs they have to do. If all the jobs are taken in turn, some will be done better by some people than by others. There will be disagreements about this. How can these be tackled? You might set up some deliberate disagreements that they need to sort out.

## A division of opinion

What happens if there are two quite different points of view in the group, with about the same number of people in each group? Do they have to reach and stick to a majority view or can people do different things? How important is it to stick together?

## Splitting up

What happens if one or two people decide to leave the group? Are they allowed to? Who will do the work that they had been doing? Will they be able to rejoin the group later? Encourage a couple of children to express dissatisfaction with the group and to announce that they are leaving. How will the rest of the group cope with this decision?

## Do we need rules?

Ask each group to think if they need to set up rules to make sure things are fair. What sort of rules do they need? Can they agree on a list of rules? Are they clear enough? Does everyone in the group have to agree before the rules can be made or is a majority enough?

## Do we need a leader?

Some groups may already have selected a leader; others may have meetings where everyone shares in the decisions. Do the groups need a leader? How should leaders be chosen? Are there limits to their power? Can they be changed and how?

## Time out

What do the children do in their spare time on the island? Can they go off and explore on their own? Or must they always stay together for safety? Do there have to be rules for leisure activities? Why? What rules?

## When the rules are broken

Ask one member of each group to do something antisocial (such as take more than their fair share of food) and then to deny having done so. What will the rest of the group do about this? How can they tell if an individual has broken the rules? How do they find out if a person is guilty or not?

## Changing the rules

Try to set up a situation where one of the group's rules will not work fairly. Do the group want to change their rule? How do they change it? Can they change it whenever they want to and, if so, how does anyone know what the rules are?

## Finishing point

How do the group eventually get off the island? Do they want to? Will they try to escape or will they try hard not to be rescued? Can they come to a majority decision?

# PHOTOCOPIABLES

The pages in this section can be photocopied and adapted to suit your own needs and those of your class. They do not need to be declared in respect of any photocopying licence. Each photocopiable page relates to a specific activity or suggestion in the main body of the book and the appropriate activity and page references are given above each photocopiable sheet.

In the card factory, page 31

What I like, page 87

Get well soon

Farming life, page 119

reservoir

pasture

dam

settlement

fields

pasture

river

187

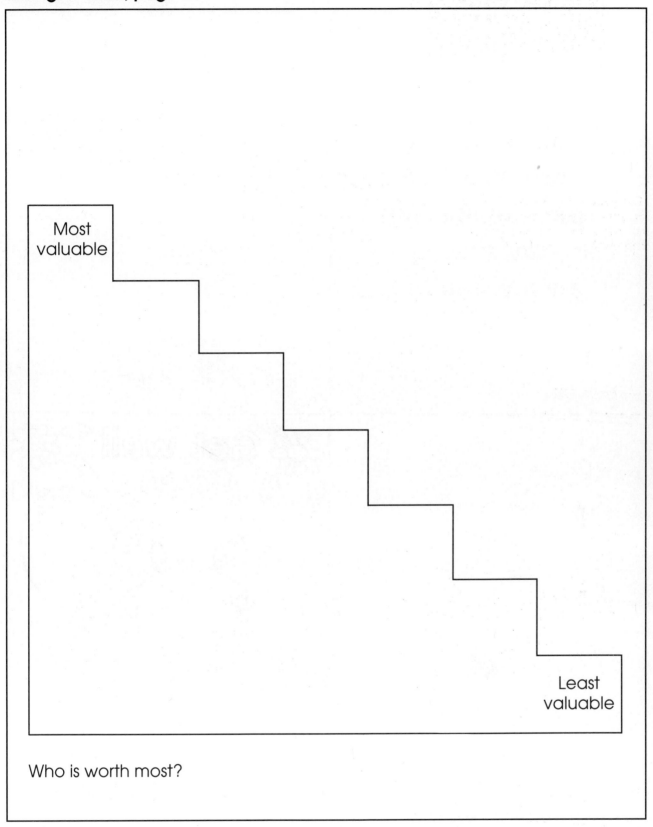

Most
valuable

Least
valuable

Who is worth most?

Hoping you are
better soon -
looking forward
to seeing you
back in action.

Get well
soon

Cut out exact shapes according to measurements.
Each is worth the value shown in the circle.

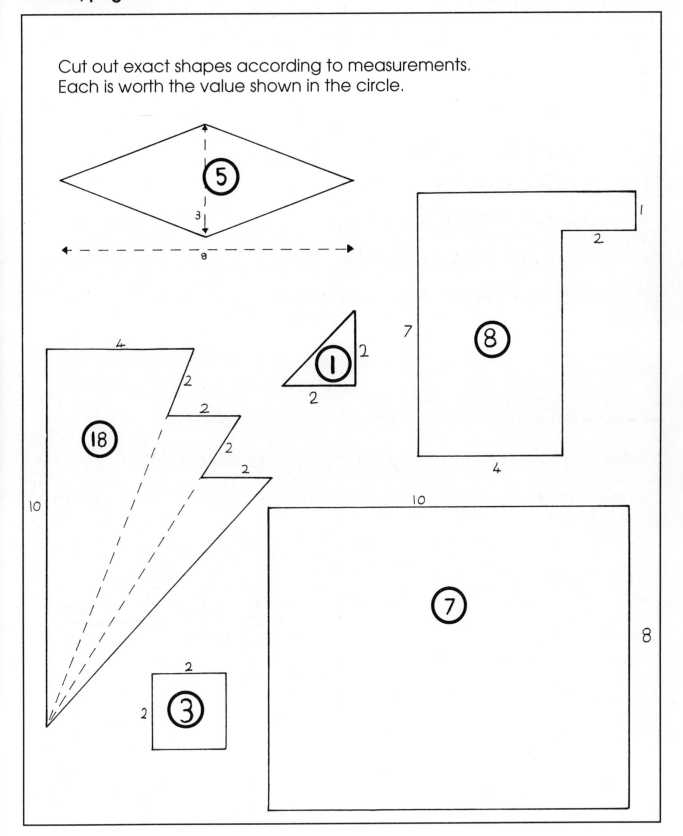

## Questionnaire for the public

Fill in this box before the interview.

Male/Female

Age: under 20 ☐    20-40 ☐    40-60 ☐    over 60 ☐

Location _____ Date _____ Time _____

We are making a survey of people's opinions on the hours shops should stay open. Would you mind if we asked you a few questions?

Do you think that shopping hours in this area are
too long ☐    about right ☐    too short? ☐

Would you like some shops to be open until later in the evening?
Yes ☐    No ☐

If yes, which of the following would you like to stay open late?

- chemists                • newsagents        • supermarkets

- household stores      • shoe shops        • banks/building societies

How late do you think they should stay open? _____

Should shops open
earlier in the morning?  Yes ☐    No ☐    If yes, how early? _____

Do you think shops should be allowed to open on Sundays?
Yes ☐    No ☐

Do you think it fair that shops which stay open for long hours should charge a little more for the goods they sell?
Yes ☐    No ☐

Thank you for your help.

### Questionnaire for shop workers

Fill in this box before the interview.

Male/Female

Age:under 20 ☐     20-40 ☐     40-60 ☐     over 60 ☐

Location _____     Date _____     Time _____

We are making a survey of shop workers' opinions on the hours shops should stay open. Would you mind if we asked you a few questions?

What are the opening hours for this shop?
Monday - Friday _____ to _____
(half day)      _____ to _____
Saturday       _____ to _____
Sunday         _____ to _____

What hours do you personally usually work?
Monday - Friday _____ to _____
(half day)      _____ to _____
Saturday       _____ to _____
Sunday         _____ to _____

Do you think that shopping hours in this shop are
too long ☐     about right ☐     too short? ☐

Would you like this shop to be open until later in the evening?
Yes ☐   No ☐

At what time would you like the shop to close? _____

Should the shop open earlier in the morning?  Yes ☐     No ☐
If yes, how early? _____

Do you think shops should be allowed to open on Sundays?  Yes ☐   No ☐

Thank you for your help.

Make a set of cards to be cut out, with one of these names on each card.

| | | |
|---|---|---|
| Aspirin | Cough mixture | Whisky |
| Cocaine | Ecstasy | Caffeine |
| Nicotine | Vitamin C tablets | Cornflakes (with added vitamins) |
| Indigestion tablets | Sun cream | Morphine |
| Anti-malarial pills | Cough pastilles | Paracetamol |
| Benzedrine | Opium | Heroin |

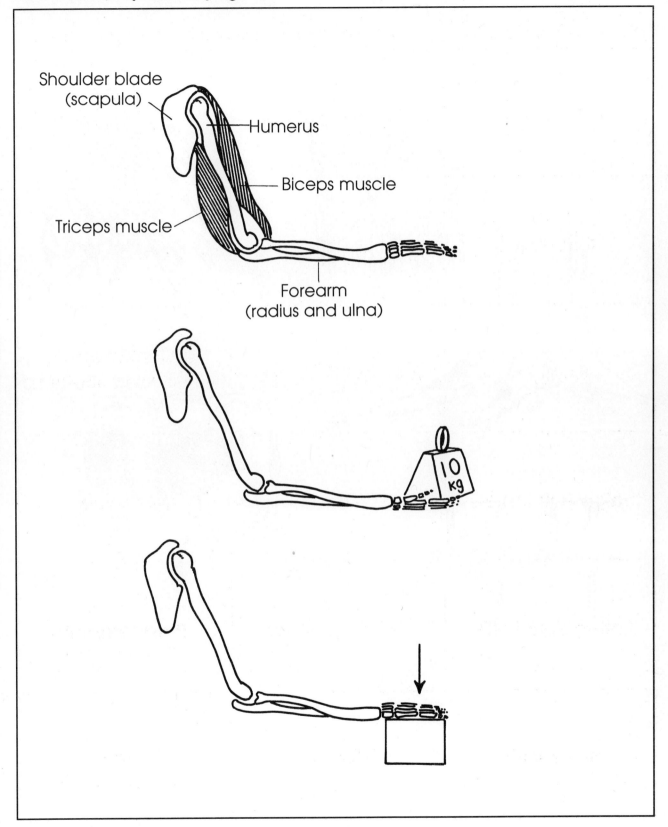

Shoulder blade
(scapula)

Humerus

Biceps muscle

Triceps muscle

Forearm
(radius and ulna)

10
kg

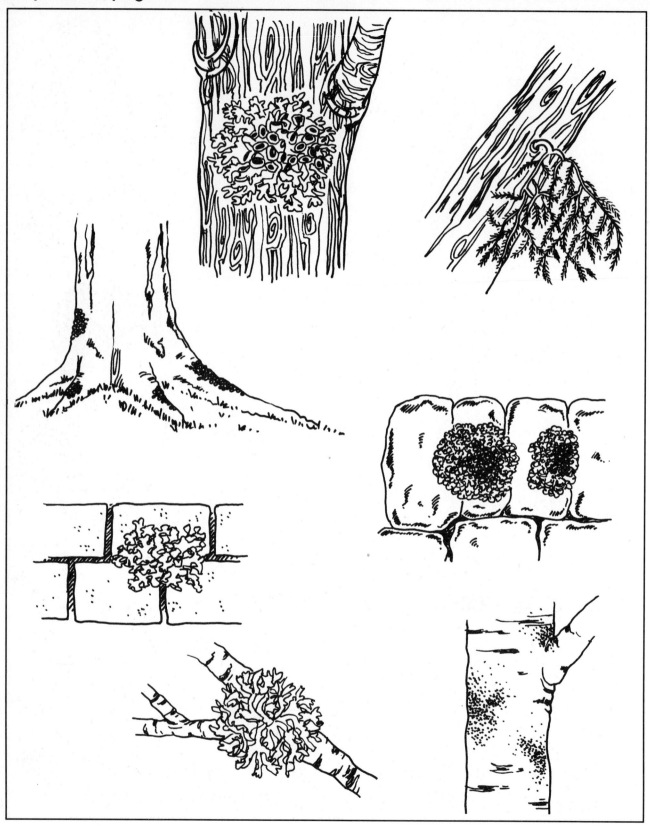

# What I like, page 87

# Target-setting

How good are you at each of the skills listed in the table below? Use the following code to show what you think.

***** very good
**** good
*** about average
** not so good
* not good

Set yourself some targets for improving some of the lowest scores over the next two weeks.

After two weeks, work with a friend to see if you have managed to meet your targets.

| Skills | Now | Two weeks later |
|---|---|---|
| Working well in a group | | |
| Explaining things to other people | | |
| Helping other people do better | | |
| Having good ideas | | |
| Solving problems | | |
| Designing things | | |
| Using computers | | |
| Writing things down | | |

| | | |
|---|---|---|
| Refuse collector | Engineer | Clothes designer |
| Builder | Headteacher | Solicitor |
| Actor | Company director | Schoolkeeper/Janitor |
| Doctor | Bus driver | Gas fitter |
| Sales assistant | Painter | Hairdresser |
| Gardener | Car maker | Cook |
| Nurse | Dancer | Oil-rig worker |
| Childminder | Teacher | Aeroplane pilot |
| Prime minister | Musician | Model |
| Crane operator | Computer operator | Soldier |
| Electrician | Secretary | Make-up artist |

**Things that I can do well**

Name _____

Solve problems

Get on with other people

Make things with my hands

Write down ideas

Explain ideas and give clear instructions

Draw plans and design things

Make pictures

Work out how to do things

Find out information

Be a good team member

# Erosion survey, page 111

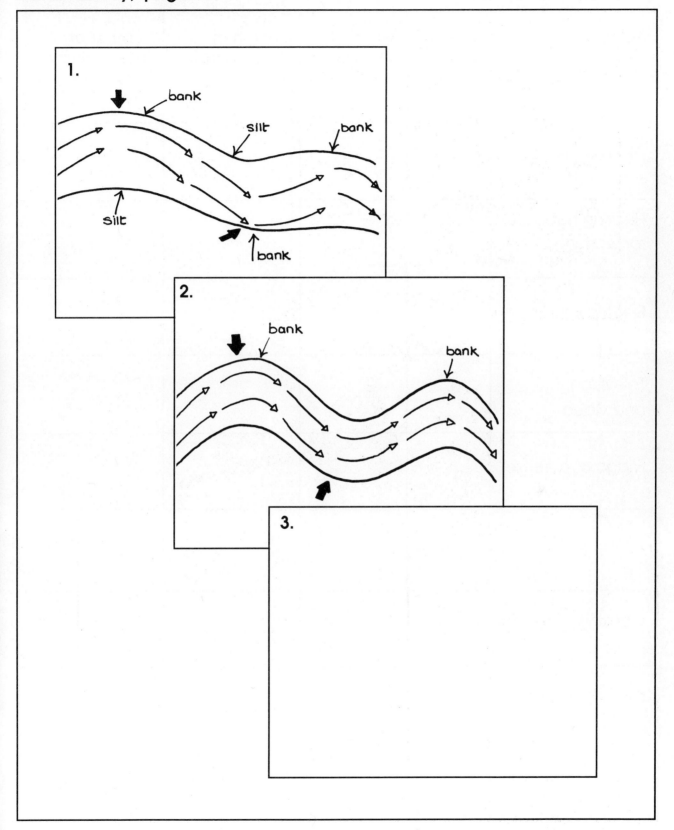

**An energy audit, page 116**

| Activity | Energy source | Amount used in 2 minutes | Length of time energy used for each activity | Number of times activity happens each day |
|---|---|---|---|---|
| Heating house | | | | |
| Heating hot water for washing | | | | |
| Electric light | | | | |
| Television and video | | | | |
| Fridge and freezer | | | | |
| Boiling kettle | | | | |
| Cooking (one ring) | | | | |
| Cooking (oven) | | | | |
| Washing machine | | | | |

# Population change, page 118

## Population growth

| Age group | This year 199... | In 10 years 200... | In 20 years 201... | In 30 years 20.... | In 40 years 20.... | In 50 years 20.... |
|-----------|------------------|--------------------|--------------------|--------------------|--------------------|--------------------|
| 0-10      | 22               |                    |                    |                    |                    |                    |
| 11-20     | 23               |                    |                    |                    |                    |                    |
| 21-30     | 25               |                    |                    |                    |                    |                    |
| 31-40     | 10               |                    |                    |                    |                    |                    |
| 41-50     | 5                |                    |                    |                    |                    |                    |
| 51-60     | 5                |                    |                    |                    |                    |                    |
| 61-70     | 3                |                    |                    |                    |                    |                    |
| 71-80     | 2                |                    |                    |                    |                    |                    |
| **Total** | 100              |                    |                    |                    |                    |                    |

## Role 1

You are an elderly person who has lived in the area all your life. You have seen times when the food supply was low and times when it was plentiful. The few crops that are sold were first planted when you were a child. The price they fetched was high when you were a young adult, but has fallen in recent years. You can remember when people got on quite well without the things that they now buy from the trader.

## Role 2

You are a young person who has been to a school and knows about the many consumer goods that might be available, if only you had the money. You have heard about new crops that might be grown, which you could sell for a good price. It would mean clearing more land and growing less foodstuffs. But you feel that you could buy extra food with the money you made.

## Role 3

You are in middle age and look after a lot of the crops – harvesting, storing and cooking. There have always been two parts to this: the food crops (which supply most of the family's needs), and the crops for selling (which are needed to get money to buy extras from the traders). The fields you tend are as large as you can cope with. You are also concerned that your water supply will only be enough for the land and animals you already have.

## Role 4

You are in middle age and tend the family's animals. These you take to pasture and milk each day. You also slaughter an animal, from time to time, to use the meat for eating and the skin for leather. You know all your animals well. There is just enough pasture land and water to keep the flock at its present size. But if there were fewer animals, the family would have less milk, meat and leather.

## Situation 1

The rains fail. There is not enough water in the dam and river to keep the fields watered and the animals fed. Do you:
**(a)** slaughter half the animals?
**(b)** stop irrigating half the fields?
**(c)** slaughter a quarter of the animals and leave a quarter of the fields?
**(d)** plant extra crops for sale, to make more cash to buy food?
**(e)** move to find a better area in which to live?

## Situation 2

The trader introduces a new crop for which he will pay very high prices. But it needs more land than you have given to your present crops for sale and also needs quite a bit of water. Do you:
**(a)** decline the offer and carry on as before?
**(b)** plant a little of the new crop (less than you used to give to the old crop)?
**(c)** plant the new crop over all your land?
**(d)** expand the area you are using for crops and plant the new crop in this area only?

## Situation 3

Locusts invade your land, eating your crops. Do you:
**(a)** spend all your money on cheap insecticide, enough to treat all the land?
**(b)** spend all your money on expensive insecticide, to treat half the land?
**(c)** move area?
**(d)** do nothing?

## Situation 4

The soil becomes less arable to produce good crops. The older people in the family say that when this has happened in the past they have opened up new fields and abandoned the old ones, usually a little at a time, over several years. Do you:
**(a)** open up two new fields this year and abandon two old ones?
**(b)** decide to move all the fields in one go and open up a whole new area?
**(c)** do nothing?
**(d)** plant just crops for sale, so that you can buy more food?

## Consequences 1

**(a)** Go short of protein, get weaker and become more prone to illness.
**(b)** Go short of carbohydrates and have much less energy.
**(c)** Go generally short of food, but not so that you are much weaker or have much less energy.
**(d)** The crops all fail, most of your animals die, and you get no extra income from selling anything.
**(e)** Everywhere you go is the same, meanwhile you have lost all your crops and most of your animals have died from drought.

## Consequences 2

**(a)** Next year, the trader gives you a still lower price for your old crops for sale. He says prices are still falling.
**(b)** Next year, you get a good harvest of the new crop and make a much bigger income.
**(c)** There is not enough water to keep all the crop going, and you have no food or materials for clothing. But you do grow enough of the new crop successfully to sell, and get enough money to buy food and clothes for next year (even though this year you have gone hungry).
**(d)** There is not enough water to keep any of the new crop going. There is no extra cash.

## Consequences 3

**(a)** You kill all the locusts, but the food crops are contaminated and make you ill, and the crops you sell are spoiled and cannot be sold.
**(b)** You keep half the land free of locusts and these crops are fine. You go hungry, but you survive.
**(c)** The locusts are everywhere. You lose all your crop.
**(d)** Lose all your crop.

## Consequences 4

**(a)** You maintain your overall food supply (no extra, but no less).
**(b)** The new fields all require more irrigation. You have not the energy or time to do this properly, so some crops fail. You go hungry.
**(c)** Next year, there is still less food and still fewer crops for sale. You must make a decision again.
**(d)** The soil is getting worn out. You grow less than you expected for sale, the price keeps going down and you have produced no food. You go very hungry!

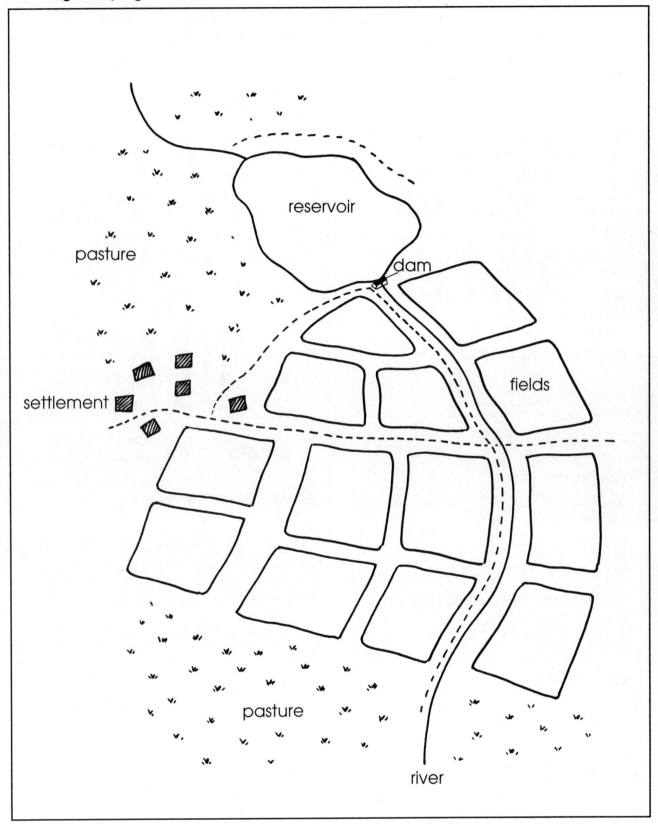

# Which groups do we belong to? page 135

**Saying 'no' to bullies, page 137**

You are on your own in the playground, nobody else is close to you. A child who is two years older than you (and bigger) demands you give them 10p or 'I'll get you into trouble.'

What do you do? _____

_____

You are with two friends leaving a sweet shop on the way home from school. A group of children stop you and tell you to share out the sweets with them – 'Two for each of us, and one for you.' There are many more of them than there are of you.

What do you do? _____

_____

You and half-a-dozen friends are playing with a ball in the playground. An older child runs off with the ball. You ask for it back, but the child refuses and runs off with it into school, which is against the rules, but no adult sees them do it. As the child goes into school he or she shouts back, 'If you tell on me, I'll thump you after school!'

What do you do? _____

_____

Walking home from school, you see three children in your class teasing a younger child from the school. The child is upset, and the teasing is beginning to get violent.

What do you do? _____

_____

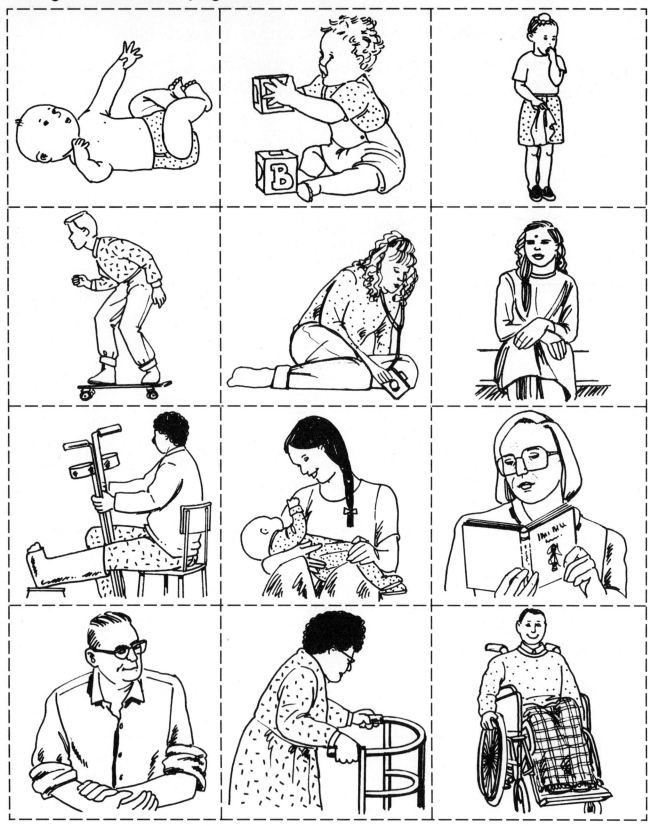

## Questionnaire on languages spoken in our school

**Note:** If the child you are interviewing is not fluent in English, ask another child who speaks that language to help you ask the questions.

Name _____

Class _____

Age _____

How well do you think you speak English?

Very well ☐   Well ☐   Fairly well ☐   Just beginning ☐   Not much ☐

What other languages do you speak?

1. _____   2. _____   3. _____

For the first of these, do you speak it:

Very well ☐   Well ☐   Fairly well ☐   Just beginning ☐   Not much ☐

For the second of these, do you speak it:

Very well ☐   Well ☐   Fairly well ☐   Just beginning ☐   Not much ☐

What languages do you usually speak at home?

1. _____   2. _____   3. _____

Can you read any of these languages?

1. Yes ☐   No ☐   2. Yes ☐   No ☐   3. Yes ☐   No ☐

Can you write any of these languages?

1. Yes ☐   No ☐   2. Yes ☐   No ☐   3. Yes ☐   No ☐

**The school that I'd like, page 148**

## Questions to think about

What is the school for?

_____

_____

Who will come to the school? (ages, how many)

_____  _____

_____  _____

_____  _____

What sort of person is needed to teach at the school?

_____

_____

_____

What things will the school need?

- books          - equipment          - teachers

- other adults   - spaces and rooms   - other facilities

_____

_____

_____